COUNTRIES
OF THE
WORLD

China

Gareth Stevens Publishing
MILWAUKEE

Goh Sui Noi, a Chinese Singaporean, has traveled frequently to China. She has worked for many years in publishing and editing.

Written by
GOH SUI NOI

Edited by
DINAH LEE

Designed by
SHARIFAH FAUZIAH

Picture research by
SUSAN JANE MANUEL

First published in North America in 1998 by
Gareth Stevens Publishing
1555 North RiverCenter Drive, Suite 201
Milwaukee, Wisconsin 53212 USA

For a free color catalog describing
Gareth Stevens' list of high-quality books
and multimedia programs, call
1-800-542-2595 (USA) or
1-800-461-9120 (CANADA)
Gareth Stevens Publishing's
Fax: (414) 225-0377.
See our catalog, on the World Wide Web:
http://gsinc.com

© **TIMES EDITIONS PTE LTD 1998**
Originated and designed by
Times Books International
an imprint of Times Editions Pte Ltd
Times Centre, 1 New Industrial Road
Singapore 536196
http://www.timesone.com.sg/te

Library of Congress Cataloging-in-Publication Data
Goh, Sui Noi.
China / by Goh Sui Noi.
p. cm. — (Countries of the world)
Includes bibliographical references and index.
Summary: Surveys the history, culture, traditions, people, and foreign relations of the "land of the dragon," where a fifth of humanity lives.
ISBN 0-8368-2124-6 (lib.bdg.)
1. China—Juvenile literature. [1. China.] I. Title.
II. Series: Countries of the world (Milwaukee, Wis.)
DS706.G64   1998
951—dc21   97-42538

Printed in Singapore

1 2 3 4 5 6 7 8 9 02 01 00 99 98

Contents

AN OVERVIEW OF CHINA

China, the "land of the dragon," is home to one-fifth of the world's total human population. It is poised to become a major world economy as the twentieth century draws to a close and a new millennium begins. This is a far cry from China at the close of the nineteenth century, when it was known to the world as the "sick man of Asia." The nation was ravaged by corruption, natural disasters, civil strife, and foreign aggression. After the Qing dynasty collapsed in 1911, nationalists and communists fought for control.

The Chinese people managed to pull themselves out of this abyss. They made some mistakes along the way, but they have also taken great strides. This book explains China's history, dating back five thousand years, its rich culture and traditions, and tells you about its people, the descendants of the dragon.

Opposite: **Bicycles are a cheap and convenient means of transportation for most people in China, and many roads are crowded with bicycles rather than cars.**

Below: **China's Forbidden City in Beijing is a cluster of imperial palaces built in A.D. 1406–1420 during the Ming Dynasty.**

THE FLAG OF CHINA

China's flag was introduced in 1949, when the People's Republic of China was declared by the communists. It is red in color, with five yellow stars at the upper left corner: one large star is surrounded by four smaller ones in a semi-circle. The color red symbolizes revolution. The large star represents the Communist Party of China. The four smaller stars represent the Chinese people and the four sections of society — the peasants, the workers, the bourgeoisie, and the capitalists — that were to be united in carrying out communism's goals.

Geography

The Land

China is located in eastern Asia, across the Pacific Ocean from the United States and Canada. Its land area of 3.7 million square miles (9.6 million square kilometers), which is slightly bigger than the United States, makes it the third largest country in the world after Russia and Canada. The country stretches more than 3,125 miles (5,028 km) from east to west and 3,420 miles (5,503 km) from north to south. A large part of the land is made up of deserts and mountains, and only about 10 percent of the land is good for farming. It is, therefore, an agricultural accomplishment that China can grow enough to feed its own people and to export to other countries.

China shares its border with fifteen countries. These include, among others, Mongolia and Russia to the north, North Korea to the east, Myanmar (Burma) and Vietnam to the south, and India, Pakistan, and Afghanistan to the west and southwest. In the east and south, the land meets the Bo Hai, Yellow, East China, and South China seas.

Below: **Rugged mountains on the border between Qinghai and Gansu provinces.**

Mountains, Deserts, and Plains

China's terrain descends in height from west to east and can be seen as a three-step staircase. At the top of the stairs, in the southwest, is the Qinghai-Tibet Plateau, so high that it is known as the roof of the world. At 13,500 feet (4,104 meters) above sea level, it is composed of snowcapped peaks and glaciers. The major mountain ranges here are the Kunlun, Gangdise, and Himalaya. China's tallest peak is Mt. Everest, which sits on the China–Nepal border. The Chinese call it Zhumulangma Feng.

The second step is from 6,550 to 3,280 feet (1,994 to 997 m) above sea level. The Takla Makan and Gobi deserts here stretch great distances in the west and north. The grasslands of Inner Mongolia and the unusually shaped cliffs, waterfalls, and gorges of Yunnan and Guizhou are also part of this step. Near the Takla Makan Desert lies the Turfan Depression, also known as the Oasis of Fire. It is the hottest place in China, with temperatures reaching 120° Fahrenheit (49° Centigrade). The third step extends from about 3,330 to 1,660 feet (1,012 to 505 m) above sea level. This is an area of flat plains and river deltas and is the most important and most heavily populated agricultural region.

Above: **Snowcapped mountains in China's Yunnan province rise high above fields of crops growing in the valleys.**

Rivers

The largest rivers, the Yangtze and Yellow rivers, start as melting snow in the Qinghai-Tibet Plateau. The Yangtze is China's longest river, flowing for 3,915 miles (6,299 km). It is the third longest river in the world after the Nile and the Amazon, and the Chinese also call it Changjiang, or "Long River." The Yellow River, or Huanghe to the Chinese, is the country's second longest river at 3,395 miles (5,462 km). It winds its way through northern China, picking up the yellow soil that gives the river its name, before emptying into the Bo Hai sea. The soil is very fertile, and it was on the banks of this river that people first settled. The river is also known as "China's Sorrow," because it sometimes overflows its banks, washing away crops and houses and killing people.

THREE GORGES DAM

In 1994, work began on building the world's largest dam, across the Yangtze River. It will be an important source of electricity, but many people are worried about the environmental impact it will have on the river's ecology.
(A Closer Look, page 69)

Above: **Autumn landscape in Lushan, Shandong province.**

Seasons

Weather conditions vary greatly in China. Summer in the northeast is warm but short, and the people have to bear long, cold winters, when temperatures can drop to as low as 18°F (−7°C). The eastern coastal regions are warm and humid. In the southernmost areas, the weather is warm all year round. Toward the northwest, the weather is unpredictable. The Qinghai-Tibet Plateau is cold all year round, but there is plenty of sunshine.

Plants and Animals

Hundreds of years of intensive farming and more recent urban expansion have destroyed much of China's natural vegetation. Today, forests cover only 13 percent of China's land surface, but there is a great variety of plants. Among these are oaks, maples, birches, pines, and trees found only in China, such as the China cypress, silver fir, and golden larch. There are also many varieties of peonies and chrysanthemums.

China also has a great diversity of wildlife. Rare species found only in China include the giant panda, golden monkey, white-lipped deer, takin, Chinese river dolphin, and Chinese alligator. Among the rare birds in China are the red-crowned crane, mandarin duck, and golden pheasant. Giant pandas,

Below: **Jiuzhaigou nature reserve in northern Sichuan.**

Bottom: **The lesser panda, also known as the red bear cat, is a reddish-brown, long-tailed mammal similar to a raccoon. It lives in the forests of the Himalaya Mountains straddling Tibet and India.**

considered a national treasure by the Chinese, live in the remote mountain areas of Sichuan, Gansu, and Shaanxi provinces. They feed only on bamboo leaves and are threatened with extinction because the bamboo forests are shrinking. To protect its forests and wildlife, China has established more than seven hundred nature reserves. Rescue centers for animals close to extinction have also been set up. The country has succeeded in breeding more than sixty species of animals threatened with extinction.

History

Half a Million Years Ago

About five hundred thousand years ago, China was inhabited by primitive human beings. This has been established from skeletal remains, such as those of Peking Man, found in caves in China. By 5000 B.C., settlements had begun to appear along the Yellow River. The people lived in houses of earth and wood, and they made tools with polished stones.

Kings and Palaces

Chinese history began with the founding of the Xia dynasty in 2200 B.C. By then, the Chinese had begun ancestor worship, or the offer of sacrifices to the dead to make sure they had a happy afterlife. Only male descendants could make these sacrifices, so it was important for families to have a son.

In 1766 B.C., the Xia dynasty was overthrown by the Shang dynasty, which lasted until 1123 B.C. Great strides were made during this period. The people learned how to weave silk and make bronze vessels, tools, and musical instruments. They lived in walled cities and grew millet, sorghum, wheat, and rice. They also began to write on bones, tortoise shells, and bronze objects. The king was the leader of the state and governed all activities. At first, kings were elected, but kingship later became hereditary, passing from father to son.

Spring and Autumn Period

The Zhous overthrew the Shangs and ruled until 770 B.C. To strengthen their rule, the Zhous granted dukes and princes land areas to control. These territories, however, owed allegiance to the Zhou king, who held the title of *tianzi* (TIAN-zi), or son of heaven. The territories gradually grew in strength and began to exert their independence from royal control; they also fought against each other during what was known as the Spring and Autumn Period (770-476 B.C.). After many years of war, seven states survived.

The discovery of iron casting around this time led to improved farming tools, and irrigation was developed on a large scale. It was also during this period that the great Chinese philosopher, Confucius, lived and taught.

Above: **An ancient gilded bronze figure. Records of daily life have been found carved on bronze objects from the Shang dynasty.**

CONFUCIUS, THE PHILOSOPHER

Confucius believed that an individual should honor his or her parents and be loyal to them. He taught people to extend this principle to the state and its rulers as well, so there would be peace and order in society.
(*A Closer Look, page 46*)

Below: **A young boy mastering calligraphy, an ancient Chinese art.**

China Under the Emperors

In 221 B.C., the king of Qin (CHIN) defeated the other states and unified China. He called himself Qin Shihuang, or "First Emperor." The Han dynasty followed (206 B.C.–A.D. 220). China started trading with Europe via the Silk Road and Buddhism was introduced from India. The Six Dynasties period, from A.D. 220 to 589, was followed by the prosperous Tang dynasty (A.D. 618–907), in which literature and the arts flourished and printing was invented. The Song dynasty (960–1279) was weak politically, but during this period commerce grew, and paper money was introduced. Merchant ships sailed to Japan, the Malay archipelago, and India.

China was ruled by invaders from the north twice in its history: by the Mongols and the Manchurians. The Mongols established the Yuan dynasty (1271–1368), and the Manchurians, the Qing dynasty (1644–1911).

INVENTIONS AND DISCOVERIES

The Chinese invented paper in the first century B.C. They later developed the art of printing. Gunpowder was also invented by the Chinese.
(*A Closer Look, page 52*)

THE SILK ROAD

About two thousand years ago, the ancient Chinese sold silk to the Roman empire by way of the Silk Road. This was a long trade route, which followed the Great Wall, cut through the mountains to Pakistan and Afghanistan, and from there reached the countries of the Mediterranean.
(*A Closer Look, page 66*)

Left: The Silk Road is still in use today! This road is part of the former trade route, which winds through rugged terrain and harsh desert.

The Opium Wars

In 1699, the British established a trading post in Canton (Guangzhou) in southern China. They bought tea, silk, medicines, and porcelain from China and in the early 1800s began selling opium to the Chinese. The Qing government tried to ban the sale of opium, and this led to a series of wars between the Chinese and the British. China lost and had to sign a treaty ceding Hong Kong to the British. China also lost a war to Japan in 1895, and a lot of land was lost or leased to Japan and the Western powers. China was soon in debt, its people were heavily taxed, and anti-Qing movements arose. The most famous uprising was the Taiping Rebellion, which broke out in 1851 in the south and lasted ten years, weakening the Qing government.

Birth of a Republic

The Qing dynasty collapsed in 1911, and the Republic of China was established by the Nationalist Party of China, or the Kuomintang. Dr. Sun Yat-sen, a Western-educated doctor, was leader of the party, and became China's first president. However, army generals, mainly in the north of China, began to grab power for themselves, establishing themselves as warlords.

The Communist Movement Takes Root

In 1919, after World War I, the Treaty of Versailles gave land in Shandong lost to the Germans to Japan instead of returning it to the Chinese. This sparked a student protest on May 4 that spread throughout the country. Known as the May Fourth Movement, it became a platform for modernization. It was during this period, in 1921, that the Chinese communist movement was born. Sun Yat-sen died in 1925 and his colleague, Chiang Kai-shek, took over. Chiang pitted his party against the communists and tried to eliminate them.

The Sino-Japanese War

In 1931, Japan invaded China, culminating in an attack on Nanjing in 1937, which was then the Chinese capital. Chiang Kai-shek was so obsessed with his fight against the communists that he largely overlooked the Japanese threat. The Japanese killed three hundred thousand people in Nanjing and burned down one-third of the city. They finally withdrew from China after their defeat by the Allied forces in World War II in 1945. Civil war broke out afterward in China between the Kuomintang and the communists.

Above: **Statue of Chiang Kai-shek, Sun Yat-sen's colleague and a nationalist, who succeeded in unifying China by defeating the warlords in the north.**

MAY FOURTH MOVEMENT

This movement started with a protest by Beijing University students in 1919. A drive for modernization began, and there was a new interest in Western ideas. Young people wanted to free the country of its old, feudal practices, and instead provide equality for everyone.
(A Closer Look, page 54)

People's Republic of China

The communists under Mao Zedong defeated the Kuomintang in 1949 and established the People's Republic of China. The Kuomintang fled to the island of Taiwan, which they have ruled since as the Republic of China. Under Mao's leadership, the people in China started to rebuild their country. By 1953, people's lives had improved considerably. To speed up development, Mao started the Great Leap Forward in 1957, a program in which farmers were organized into communes that shared land and resources. Some people were taken out of the fields to work in small factories. In time, more attention was paid to factory production, and the fields were neglected. Alternating floods and droughts later caused a two-year famine that killed thirty million people.

TIANANMEN SQUARE INCIDENT

This public square was the site of a huge student protest in 1989. Many died when the authorities tried to stop the demonstration.
(A Closer Look, page 70)

Below: **Mao Zedong proclaiming the Republic's founding on October 1, 1949.**

Cultural Revolution

In 1966, Mao launched the Cultural Revolution to turn the Chinese from their traditional ways. Books were burned and relics were destroyed. Teachers, scientists, and engineers were thrown into prison or sent to work in the countryside. Great upheaval and grave damage to the economy resulted. The revolution ended with the death of Mao in 1976. Changes came with the leadership of Deng Xiaoping, and by 1979, reforms were launched to propel China into the modern world.

THE LOST YEARS

Both the Great Leap Forward and the Cultural Revolution caused much economic damage to the country and hindered its progress. Millions of people died as a result.
(A Closer Look, page 56)

Qin Shihuang and the Great Wall

The first emperor of China, Qin Shihuang, unified the country in 221 B.C. but is remembered as a harsh dictator. To strengthen his rule, he burned books that he disapproved of and buried alive scholars who disagreed with his views. But he also standardized weights and measures and the written language of the Chinese. He abolished the feudal system and created a central government.

Rival feudal territories had, by then, built walls around their lands to keep out invading nomads from the north. Qin Shihuang forced many men to work on joining these walls together and extending them into one long fortification that stretched for thousands of miles. Today, this colossal structure, known as the Great Wall, stands as a reminder of China's ancient civilization.

A Chinese Empress

Empress Wu Zetian (624–705) was the only woman to have ruled from the imperial throne of China. She entered the palace as a concubine at the age of thirteen and manipulated her way into the crown prince's heart. When the old emperor died, the new emperor made her his empress. When he died in 683 and their son became emperor, Wu Zetian ruled the country through her influence over her son. In 690, she ascended the throne herself, establishing the Zhou dynasty. She was a wise ruler and the country prospered.

Below: **The Great Wall stretches for 4,160 miles (6,693 km) across northern China, crossing loess plateaus, mountains, deserts, rivers, and valleys. It passes through five provinces and two autonomous regions. It was built under Qin Shihuang's rule, and prisoners, civilians, and soldiers were forced to work on it. Millions died of starvation, disease, and exhaustion.**

Sun Yat-sen

Sun Yat-sen (1866–1925) was a medical doctor educated in Hawaii and Hong Kong. He started a revolutionary movement in China, a weak and divided country at the time, and traveled the world to gather support and raise funds for his efforts, mainly from overseas Chinese. To solve China's problems, he advanced three principles: nationalism, democracy, and social well-being. Basic industries would be run by the government, and farmers would own their land. After many revolts, Manchu rule — the Qing dynasty — collapsed in 1911, and Sun became the first president of the Chinese republic. However, he gave up the presidency to a warlord who controlled much of northern China. He died in 1925, at the age of fifty-nine, without seeing China united and strong. Today, he remains an inspiration to communists and nationalists alike and is regarded as the father of modern China.

Dr. Sun Yat-sen

Mao Zedong

Mao Zedong (1893–1976) was one of the founders of the Chinese Communist Party. A brilliant military strategist, he led the communists to victory against the nationalists to establish the People's Republic of China in 1949. The period under his leadership was marked by extraordinary events. He gave women equality with men, saying that they held up "half of heaven." He also urged them into the fields and factories to work side by side with the men. A leader with great charisma, he was able to mobilize the Chinese into rebuilding their country. However, the two movements he initiated in his later years, the Great Leap Forward and the Cultural Revolution, set back the economic progress of the country and decimated its intellectual resources.

Mao Zedong

Deng Xiaoping

Deng Xiaoping (1904–1997) joined the communists when he was a student worker in France in the 1920s. He strongly believed that people should not live in poverty. He tried to rescue the country from economic chaos in the early 1960s after the disastrous Great Leap Forward, but was banished to the countryside. Shortly after Mao's death he regained power and, in 1979, introduced reforms to move China into the modern world. He also created the "one country, two systems" formula that paved the way for the return of Hong Kong to China in 1997.

Deng Xiaoping

Government and the Economy

Communist Party of China

The Chinese choose deputies to represent them at meetings and to make laws. Each deputy belongs to a people's congress in his or her town or city. Above the people's congresses is the National People's Congress. The Communist Party of China forms the government and rules the country, which is divided into provinces, autonomous regions, and municipalities.

National People's Congress

The National People's Congress holds the highest state power in China and has the power to amend the constitution and make laws. It elects the president and vice-president of the country, and approves the president's nomination of the prime minister and members of the State Council. Members, known as deputies, are elected every five years from the provinces, autonomous regions, and municipalities. They meet once a year in Beijing to decide on important issues.

Above: A farmer with his geese in China's Fujian province. Each province is further divided into cities and towns with their own local government.

Role of the President

The president is the head of state, with the power to appoint or remove members of the State Council. He also meets foreign diplomats and heads of state on behalf of the people. Currently, the president is Jiang Zemin.

State Council

The governments of the provinces, autonomous regions, and municipalities report to the State Council, headed by the prime minister. The State Council consists of ministries and state commissions. Some of its functions include building schools, training doctors and nurses, and maintaining law and order.

Above: **A school in Sichuan province. Education and health matters come under the jurisdiction of the State Council, which functions as the central government.**

Central Military Commission

The Central Military Commission commands the armed forces of China, which includes the Chinese People's Liberation Army, Chinese People's Armed Police Force, and the militia.

The Judiciary

The Supreme People's Court and various people's courts try civil and criminal cases. The Supreme People's Procuratorate and the people's procuratorates oversee legal proceedings.

Regional and Local Governments

China is divided into twenty-three provinces, five autonomous regions, and four municipalities, each with its own regional government that reports to the State Council. The provinces and autonomous regions are further divided into cities and towns, each having its own government that reports to the regional government. The five autonomous regions are Inner Mongolia, Ningxia, Xinjiang, Guangxi, and Tibet, where many minority people live. The four municipalities are Beijing, Shanghai, Tianjin, and Chongqing.

Farming

Most Chinese are farmers; they make up 74 percent of China's population. Although China is vast, only 10 percent of the land can be cultivated; the rest is desert and mountains. In the north, where the climate is dry and summer short, people grow crops that do not need much water; these include wheat, corn, sorghum, and millet. In the south, where the weather is warmer and rainfall is abundant, rice is the main crop. Here, pigs and poultry are more common than sheep and goats because of a lack of grazing land.

MIDNIGHT HANDOVER

After 155 years of British rule, Hong Kong reverted to China on July 1, 1997. It now holds the status of "Special Administrative Region" within China.

(A Closer Look, page 58)

Below: **Buying wool at a market in one of the minority regions.**

Above: **Site of the Three Gorges Dam on the Yangtze River.**

Mineral Resources and Industry

China has rich mineral resources, including coal, iron ore, oil, tin, copper, and bauxite. The mining industry, therefore, is very important. China exports some of these minerals. The country makes its own airplanes, ships, automobiles, and machinery, as well as electrical appliances and other consumer goods. It exports textiles, garments, toys, telecommunications and recording equipment, oil, and minerals. It imports specialized industrial machinery, chemicals, manufactured goods, steel, yarn, textiles, and fertilizers.

Energy Needs and Transportation

China needs a great deal of energy to fuel its industrial development. It is therefore exploiting its immense hydroelectric power potential and is building the world's largest dam across the swift-flowing Yangtze River. It is also building nuclear power plants. New railways are being constructed and multiple-lane expressways built to link major cities. River transport remains important. The building of the Three Gorges Dam on the Yangtze is expected to improve the "golden waterway" of China by slowing down the flow of water and increasing the depth of the river in its upper reaches, so allowing ships to travel farther up the river.

ECONOMIC REFORMS

In 1979, China started economic reforms to improve people's lives. Government control was reduced, and farmers are now allowed to sell excess produce in private markets. People can also set up small businesses.

(A Closer Look, page 48)

People and Lifestyle

One Child Per Couple

China is the most populous country in the world with 1.2 billion people, or 20 percent of the world's population. It is multicultural and has fifty-six ethnic groups. With such a large population, China faces problems of overcrowding. Since the 1980s, government policy has required couples living in cities to have only one child. In rural areas, a couple may have a second child under special circumstances, such as a labor shortage on the farm. Ethnic minorities may have more than one child.

Han Chinese

This is the largest ethnic group in China, with about one billion people. The Han Chinese are found in all parts of the country, but live mainly along the Yellow and Yangtze rivers and in the northeastern plain. They speak different dialects in different regions. To communicate, they speak *putonghua* (PU-TONG-hua) or Mandarin, which is actually a dialect of northern China.

OVERSEAS CHINESE

Today, ethnic Chinese live in countries all over the world, many of them born in the countries they now call home.
(*A Closer Look, page 62*)

Below: Family planning became a state policy in 1982, and a one-child family is the norm in the cities.

Minority Groups

The other fifty-five ethnic groups are scattered in the border regions in the north, northeast, northwest, southeast, and southwest. Most live in autonomous regions that are self-governing. They have their own spoken languages, and twenty-three have their own written languages.

Mongolians and Kazakhs inhabit the grasslands of the north and northwest. They are nomads who move their sheep, cattle, and horses from place to place in search of pastures. They live in round tents called yurts. Both the Mongolians and Kazakhs are good horsemen. They eat dairy products and mutton, and enjoy tea with milk. The Mongolians are mainly Buddhists, and the Kazakhs are Muslims. The Tibetans in the southwest are either herdsmen or farmers who practice Lamaism, which is a form of Buddhism.

Many of the other groups in the southwest, as well as those in the south and southeast, are farmers. The Zhuangs in the southwest grow crops such as rice, sugarcane, bananas, and corn. They are also famous for their brocade embroidery. The Li people in the southeast island of Hainan are farmers, but they also produce goods such as textiles, machinery, and electrical goods.

Above: **A Kazakh family in their tent. The extended family usually includes grandparents and even uncles and aunts.**

UNDERSTANDING TIBET

The Tibetans believe in reincarnation, in which a person may die physically but the soul is reborn into a new body.
(A Closer Look, page 72)

Rich and Poor

China's wealthy are concentrated in the cities, while its poorest citizens live in the countryside. Rural people are less educated than those who live in the cities because many children, especially girls, drop out of school to work on the farms. Farmers and their families often leave the poverty of the rural areas and go to the cities to look for work. This has created housing and employment problems for the government.

Family Structure

Life in China revolves around the family: children, parents, and often the paternal grandparents live together. With the government's one-child family policy, children are regarded as precious and they are doted on. Sons are often favored over daughters because they carry on the family name and look after the parents in their old age. In a Chinese family, respect for an elder person is very important, even if the age difference is small. So a younger sibling does not address an older one by name, but as *jiejie* (JIEH- jieh) for elder sister, or *gege* (KERH-kerh) for elder brother. Children are expected always to obey their parents.

Below: **A woman with her grandson. In the traditional family structure, elderly couples live with one of their sons and his family. The eldest son is usually preferred because he has a moral obligation to look after his parents in their old age.**

Marriage and Children

Marriages in China used to be arranged for the bridal couple by their parents. Today, young people prefer to choose their own partners. On the wedding day, the groom, dressed in a Western-style suit and tie, goes to the bride's home in a limousine decorated with flowers and ribbons. He escorts the bride to his home. She is usually dressed in a white bridal gown. The main celebration is a lunch or dinner banquet at a restaurant, which includes a very simple ceremony. After marriage, a woman continues to work until she has a child. Women in the cities have maternity leave lasting from two months to a year, but women in rural areas may have to return to the fields to work much earlier.

Daily Life

Most Chinese workers belong to a *danwei* (TAHN-way), or work unit, that provides housing, child care, education, and other facilities. A large corporation or a group of factories can make up one danwei. Most Chinese women work outside the home, so their children are looked after by the grandparents or are placed in child care centers.

Above: **In rural areas, women often work on the farm or sell homemade goods to supplement the family's income.**

HOLDING UP HALF THE SKY

Through most of China's history, women were regarded as inferior to men. It was only under communist rule that the role of women was recognized. Women now work in many professions in China.
(A Closer Look, page 50)

Old Age

After retirement, an elderly couple may become babysitters for their grandchild. When they have the time, they go to the park for some exercise or just to chat with friends. Some keep busy with community work, such as serving in neighborhood groups that look after the residents' needs. Life is not lonely, and they can expect their children to take care of them in their old age.

Elementary Education

Children in the cities start school at the age of six, but those in small towns and rural areas start at the age of seven. City children go to school six days a week. Classes start at eight in the morning and end at five in the evening, with a two-hour lunch break at midday. Subjects taught include Chinese, arithmetic, physical education, music, fine arts, moral education, science, history, and geography. In remote areas, there are sometimes no schools at all, or they are located so far away that a child may have to walk for up to three hours to get to his or her school. Besides academic subjects, some rural schools teach practical skills such as tailoring, weaving, cooking, crop planting, and animal husbandry.

Below: **Lunch being served to a group of preschool children, who learn basic speech patterns and counting during play.**

Left: **A high school student uses a computer under the watchful eye of his teacher.**

High School

After six years of elementary school, children go to high school, which is divided into three years of junior high and three years of senior high. After junior high, students can choose to go to a general, vocational, or technical school. After school hours, the students may join clubs where the activities range from community service to music and painting. In vocational schools, students learn skills such as tailoring, building, preschool teaching, photography, accounting, and electronics.

Higher Education

During the start of the Cultural Revolution, schools and colleges were closed. While many elementary and high schools reopened in 1967, universities and colleges were slower to do so. Some did not open until after the Cultural Revolution was over. In recent years, however, university education has become a priority.

After senior high school, students who want to attend a university take a national entrance examination. They may choose a comprehensive university, a teachers' university, or a specialized institution that concentrates on fields such as science, engineering, economics, fine arts, or music. This examination, carried out over three days in early July, is a time of great anxiety for those who aspire to a higher education.

LITERACY DRIVE

At the beginning of the twentieth century, only 15 percent of the Chinese population could read or write. After the People's Republic of China was set up in 1949 under communist rule, primary education became available for all children, and adult education was introduced to increase literacy among older people. Today, more than 75 percent of China's population over the age of twelve can read and write.

Taoism and Buddhism

Many Chinese still cling to a set of ancient beliefs combined with Taoist and Buddhist influences. Taoism is an indigenous religion of China that teaches people to live in harmony with their natural surroundings. The Taoists meditate, keep to a vegetarian diet, and perform breathing exercises; they also use magic and spells. *Taijiquan* (TAI-chi-CHUAN), a form of shadow-boxing, and *qigong* (CHI-kohng), a breathing exercise, were developed by the Taoists. Buddhism was brought to China by Indian merchants in the first century B.C. and spread widely after A.D. 4. Chinese Buddhism, known as Chan Buddhism, is a fusion of Taoist and other Chinese beliefs with Indian Buddhism. Another form of Chinese Buddhism, Lamaism, is practiced by the Tibetans and Mongolians.

SECRET SOCIETIES

Secret societies have been around for many centuries in China. Most were started by peasants discontented with their poverty and in rebellion against the government. Today, such organizations still exist, even though they have been outlawed in China and in other countries.

(A Closer Look, page 64)

Left: **A Taoist temple in Xiamen. Offerings can be made to a number of different deities in the Chinese pantheon of gods.**

Folk Beliefs

Many Chinese believe in gods and lesser spirits, such as the spirits of mountains and lakes. The people aim to live in harmony with the spirits and avoid offending them, or else find ways to appease the angry ones. Ancestor worship is another ancient custom based on the belief that the dead go to another world. It is the duty of the living to take care of dead ancestors, so paper "money" is burned as an offering, and food is placed at graves.

Islam

Islam arrived in China in A.D. 7. Minority ethnic groups such as the Uighurs and Kazakhs are Muslims, but the biggest group of Muslims are the Huis, who number more than seven million.

Christianity

The first Christians to arrive in China were the Nestorians, who arrived from Syria in A.D. 635. They were followed by the Jesuits during the thirteenth century, while Roman Catholic and Protestant missionaries started arriving in the nineteenth century. However, Christianity made little impact on the Chinese, and followers of the faith are concentrated only in cities such as Beijing and Shanghai.

Above: **A mosque located on the northern bank of the Yellow River caters to the Hui minority group, which is Muslim.**

Language and Literature

Mandarin

Minority ethnic groups have their own spoken, and sometimes written, language. Among the Han Chinese, people in different regions speak their own dialects. However, everyone learns to speak Mandarin at school, and it is the language used to communicate with others. The people call Mandarin putonghua, or "the common language."

Written Language

Although many Chinese dialects exist, they share one written script. Formed about six thousand years ago, the Chinese script is the oldest form of writing in the world that is still in use today. It has no alphabet; instead, a pictorial character is used for a word. There are more than fifty thousand words, or characters. About three thousand are used daily.

The ancient Chinese began expressing their ideas in drawings, which became simpler and stylized over time. For example,

Below: **Comic books are popular in China. This streetside comics library attracts avid readers.**

Above: **These bold, red, Mandarin words on the wall behind the barber are a call to socialism.**

the character for *che* (CHERH), or vehicle, began as the drawing of a chariot but evolved to become only a representation of the original drawing. In 1964, the government simplified the script further by reducing the number of written strokes. To make the language more understandable for non-Chinese, *pinyin* (PIN-yin), or the translating of Chinese words into Romanized script, was developed.

Literature

China has a rich literary history; the earliest anthology of poetry, *The Book of Songs*, was compiled in 600 B.C., and contains 305 poems. Three hundred years later, during the Warring States period, Qu Yuan, China's first great poet, wrote *Li Sao* ("LI-SAO"), or *The Lament*, a lyrical poem still read today. Some of the greatest poetry was written during the Tang and Song dynasties. Drama developed during the Yuan dynasty, but the first novels appeared during the subsequent Ming dynasty. In the 1920s, writers began to write in the everyday language of the people, instead of in classical Chinese. After the communist revolution, literature was used to serve the communist cause by glorifying the working class.

Arts

Western Influence

China's artistic traditions date back thousands of years. At the turn of the twentieth century, however, when the country struggled with its domestic problems, Chinese artists looked to the West for inspiration. After the communist takeover, the arts were suppressed, and folk artists had to turn away from traditional themes to social ones, such as glorifying revolutionaries and workers. Today, artists have more freedom to do what they want.

Above: **Handpainted combs in the vibrant colors favored by Chinese folk artists.**

Painting Techniques

In traditional Chinese painting, the artist paints on paper or silk. His tools are the brush, ink, and paint made from mineral or plant pigments. Brush strokes are important, and a painter may take years to perfect his strokes. The painter's subjects are human figures, landscapes, flowers, birds, fish, insects, and other animals. Today, some Chinese painters have blended the techniques of traditional Chinese painting with those of Western painting.

Below: **This Chinese wall painting hangs in the summer palace of the Dalai Lama in Lhasa, Tibet.**

Chinese opera began as street entertainment, and gongs, cymbals, and drums were used to attract an audience. Today, these instruments are still used to introduce each new scene.

Left: This elaborately dressed character is a warrior in an opera. He carries the four flags of his regiment behind him; they can also serve as weapons. Stories featured in Chinese opera may be comic or tragic and are usually taken from historical epics, folk legends, classical novels, or fairy tales. Each performance may last two or three hours.

Chinese Opera

There are at least three hundred forms of traditional opera in China; some of the more popular ones are the Beijing, Yue, Ping, and Yu opera styles. The stage is usually bare except for a few pieces of furniture placed against a painted backdrop. The actors wear glittering costumes and headdresses, and the details of their thick makeup tell the audience whether a character is upright or dishonest, kind or cruel, or a clown. As there are few props, many of the actions, such as opening a door or rowing a boat, are mimed. Most of the dialogue is sung, and acrobatics are included in some forms of opera.

Cinema

The Chinese began to make movies in the 1920s and were influenced by Russian and American films. Like all other art forms, movie-making suffered during the Cultural Revolution and only began to flourish again in the 1980s. Some of the better works have won international acclaim.

Rhythms and Melodies

Different regions of China have their own rhythms and melodies. Most Chinese music has a symbolic or descriptive theme, such as a famous battle, flying geese, a harvest, or feelings of joy or grief. It may also mimic bird calls or a running brook. Traditionally, music was played at weddings, funerals, and other occasions. It played an important part in Chinese social life but this is much less true today.

Chinese music has been influenced by foreign music from the earliest times. For example, the pipa and the *huqin* (HOO-chin), a type of violin, came from Central Asia. Chinese instruments include the flute, lute, violin, zither, gong, cymbals, and drums. Today's Chinese orchestra might also include the Western violin, cello, or double bass.

Top: **Musicians of the Dai minority group in Yunnan. Most Chinese music has a symbolic or descriptive theme, focusing on different emotions, or events, such as battles or the time of harvest.**

Above: **China's best-known movie actress, Gong Li.**

Architectural Style

The traditional Chinese building is rectangular in shape and consists of several units separated by open courtyards. It is usually surrounded by a high wall for privacy. What is most distinctive is the roof, which slopes downward and then turns up at the corners.

Folk Crafts

Embroidery has been refined into an art, and Chinese women embroider flower and animal motifs on clothes, shoes, purses, tablecloths, and bed linens. The Chinese also use a dough mixture of rice and wheat to make figures of mythological characters. They paint these with colorful dyes and mount them on bamboo splints.

Left: **Chinese embroidery is always intricate and colorful. Traditionally, girls learn the skill from their mothers at a young age.**

PAPER-CUTTING

On festive occasions, women and children cut pieces of red paper into designs to decorate the windows, doors, and walls of their homes. For weddings, a pair of mandarin ducks and the written character for double happiness are favorite motifs. The art of paper-cutting began during the Han dynasty as a pastime of the rich court ladies, because paper in those days was a highly prized item. Over time, paper-cutting has become a part of folk culture.

Leisure and Festivals

More Money, Less Time

Recent economic reforms by the government have created greater wealth among the Chinese. This means they have more money to spend on recreation, but ironically they may have less time for fun. Employers are making greater demands on their workers, and people are willing to work harder for better rewards. This does not mean, however, that the Chinese do not enjoy their leisure activities.

Recreation

After a day's work, people in the city may go to a cinema or karaoke lounge, enjoy a meal out, or simply return home to watch television. They also like to visit their relatives and friends, and usually show up unannounced. The Chinese are used to having visitors drop by without prior notice. If the visit happens to coincide with their meal time, they just set an extra place at the table and invite the guest to join in; otherwise, they chat over tea and snacks.

Below: **People performing Western ballroom dances on a Shanghai sidewalk. Sidewalks and closed-off streets are a frequent spot for evening dances. Western music is also gaining popularity with the younger generation.**

Bowling is popular in China, and bowling alleys are well-frequented by young people. The young also like to go to discotheques, but older people prefer ballroom dancing. In the evenings, sections of streets are sometimes closed off so people can dance. Parks are a favorite place for the Chinese. Older people go to parks to play a game of cards or chess, or simply to chat with their friends. Owners of song birds take them to the park, where their singing skills can be compared with other birds.

In rural areas, work on the farm takes up most of the time, but adults may play a game of cards as recreation, while children play games they invent themselves. They also watch television if the family can afford one. Hardworking adults may spend their evening hours sewing quilts or weaving baskets for sale.

Children

Children spend a lot of time on homework, but when time permits they play games such as jump rope, hopscotch, hide-and-seek, and tag. Many boys and girls like to kick a type of shuttlecock — a heavy round rubber pad topped with feathers — and they enjoy playing video games in arcades.

Traditional Sports

The people who perform morning exercises in parks do not do aerobics, but instead use physical movements that the Chinese have been doing for hundreds of years. Of the many traditional sports, the three most popular are taijiquan, or shadowboxing; qigong, a breathing exercise; and *wushu* (WU-shu), self-defense. There are regional and national competitions in all of these.

In taijiquan, the mind guides the body through a set of movements that are slow and graceful, yet purposeful. The movements are combined with deep breathing, and the result is a feeling of calmness. Qigong is a deep-breathing exercise aimed at helping a person stay alert, live longer, and overcome diseases. People believe that it helps to strengthen bodily functions through the control of *qi* (CHI), a form of energy flowing through the human body. Wushu is a self-defense art that involves hand-to-hand combat or fighting with weapons such as swords, spears, and sabers. It is known in the West as *gongfu* (GONG-foo) and has been popularized by the many action movies from Hong Kong.

Among the minority groups, the Mongolians enjoy wrestling and horseback riding, while the Tibetans like yak racing.

THE ART OF HEALING

The Chinese believe that illness is caused by an imbalance of the body's energy flow. So besides exercising to promote health, they rely on a system of herbal remedies to maintain or restore the body's state of well-being.
(*A Closer Look*, page 44)

Below: It is a common sight to see people performing their taijiquan exercise outdoors, where friends and neighbors can meet, and where space is less confined than in their homes.

Above: **Young people play ping-pong at the People's Stadium in Sichuan province.**

Mass Sports

In school, physical exercise is part of the curriculum, and students may also be required to do eye exercises between lessons. At work, there are 15-minute breaks in the morning and afternoon for physical exercise and sports. Schools, factories, and government organizations provide sports facilities such as basketball courts and ping-pong (table tennis) tables. The Chinese enjoy swimming in lakes and rivers when the weather permits, and they go ice-skating in winter. Where sports facilities are not available, they improvise so that a quiet lane may serve as a badminton court, and any table may be used to play ping-pong.

Competitive Sports

In 1984 in Los Angeles, China celebrated its return to the Olympic Games by winning fifteen gold, eight silver, and nine bronze medals. It was the first time China had ever won a gold medal in the Olympics. China had withdrawn from the Games in 1956 to protest Taiwan's participation. Since its 1984 success, China has done increasingly well in international sports, particularly in swimming, diving, gymnastics, track and field, badminton, and ping-pong. They have set world records in track and field events and swimming.

TRAINING POTENTIAL SPORTS CHAMPIONS

Children who show promise in sports are enrolled in special sports schools at a young age. Sometimes, this means being separated from their families and going to strange and faraway places. At the school, they spend most of their time training, but they also take lessons in academic subjects.

Spring Festival

Each year, at the beginning of spring, the Chinese usher in the new lunar year with a big celebration. The Spring Festival, or Lunar New Year, falls between late January and early February, but preparations begin much earlier. People give their houses a thorough spring cleaning, replace old furnishings, hang decorations, buy or sew new clothing, repay their debts, and make sure their rice bins and larders are well-stocked. This ensures good fortune for the coming year.

Perhaps the most important day of the festival is the eve of the New Year, when families have a reunion dinner. Children who live away from home try to return for this dinner, during which special foods are prepared and eaten. After dinner, family members sit together to talk or play games until the early hours of the morning. The next day, people wear their new clothes to visit relatives and friends. Bright colors are worn, particularly red because it is an auspicious, or lucky, color. Children receive *hongbao* (HOHNG-pao), or gifts of money in envelopes that are also red. Lion and dragon dances and stilt-walking performances take place in parks and other open areas, and celebrations may continue for two weeks.

Top and *above:* Stilt-walkers and colorfully decorated tangerine trees are always part of Lunar New Year celebrations. These trees are considered a symbol of good fortune because of the lucky golden color of the fruit.

Tomb-Sweeping Day

Qingmingjie (CHING-ming jieh), which translates as "clear and bright festival," occurs on April 5. Also called Tomb-Sweeping Day, it is a day when people remember their ancestors by sweeping their tombs clean and paying their respects to the deceased. Burial grounds are usually in the countryside, so a visit often becomes a family outing, with a picnic meal and kite-flying to lend the occasion a festive mood. It is also a time to enjoy the beauty of spring.

Dragon Boat Festival

This festival falls on the fifth day of the fifth lunar month and celebrates the memory of a patriotic poet named Qu Yuan. The poet drowned himself in a river when his state was conquered by another. Tradition has it that villagers threw rice dumplings into the river to prevent the fish from devouring the poet's body while they tried to recover it. The event is remembered by holding dragon boat races (boats with a dragon-head on the bow), and eating rice dumplings stuffed with meat and wrapped in bamboo leaves.

Mid-Autumn Festival

On the fifteenth day of the eighth lunar month, when the harvest moon is at its brightest, the Chinese gather to enjoy the sight of the moon and eat special cakes made for the occasion. The cakes are usually round, like the full moon, and filled with lotus seed paste. The Chinese call the festival *Zhongqiujie* (CHONG-chiu jieh), and children carry lanterns in the street on this night.

Minority Festivals

Ethnic minorities in China have their own festivals. For example, the Dais in Yunnan province hold a water-splashing festival in the spring. During this festival, people splash water on each other to wash away ill fortune and give showers of blessings.

The Zhuangs have a cattle-soul festival in spring after the fields have been plowed. Family members carry a basketful of steamed, five-colored glutinous rice, and a bundle of fresh grass to the cattle pen. A sacrificial rite is performed there, after which the rice and grass are fed to the cattle. The Zhuangs believe that striking the cattle during plowing causes their souls to flee; the ritual is held to call the souls back.

Above: **Dais in Yunnan province use water pistols to drench each other during a New Year festival.**

LUNAR CALENDAR

While the Chinese use the Western calendar in their daily lives today, they have had their own calendar for thousands of years. In the Chinese lunar calendar, there are twelve months to a year, and each month begins with a new moon. Traditional festivals are celebrated according to the Chinese calendar, and it is still referred to for important events, such as setting the date of a wedding, opening a business, or moving into a new house.

Food

Rice and Other Food

The Chinese divide food into *fan* (FAHN), or grain, which may be rice or wheat, and *cai* (chai), which literally means vegetables. But *cai* also refers to all other non-grains, including fish and meat. In south China, the primary grain is rice, which grows well in the wet climate. Wheat is grown in the north, where it is made into bread, noodles, and dumplings. Southerners eat mainly pork and poultry, while northerners eat more mutton. Fish is consumed when it is available. Meals include a soup, and a serving of tea.

There are many cooking methods. Rice, noodles, and dumplings are boiled; breads and buns are steamed. Meat and vegetables are steamed, simmered, deep-fried, stir-fried, smoked, blanched, or boiled. Cooking utensils include the versatile cleaver, which is a flat, broad knife blade, with a handle that is used to hack bones, mince meat, slice fish, chop garlic, crush ginger, and even mash beans. The wok, a pan in the shape of a half sphere, can be used to deep-fry, stir-fry, boil, simmer, and steam food.

THE ORIGIN OF TEA DRINKING

Tea drinking started in China nearly five thousand years ago. It found its way to the West in the seventeenth century.
(*A Closer Look*, page 60)

Below: Chinese food offers a multitude of flavors and a large variety of regional cuisines.

Regional Flavors

People in different parts of China cook their food differently, but there are five main regional cuisines. Northerners in and around Beijing use a lot of garlic, chilies, and oil in their food. In Henan, in the Yellow River basin, sweet and sour food is favored and eaten with pancakes and bread. People in the east, in and around Zhejiang province, consume rice with fresh fish and shellfish that are steamed or cooked in soy sauce and sugar. People in the south cook their food lightly in very little seasoning to enjoy its full flavor. In western China, particularly in Sichuan province, food is cooked in hot spices. Among the minorities, the Uighurs and Kazakhs eat crusty pancakes with roast mutton kebab. Mongolians drink tea with milk, while Tibetans like buttered tea.

Meal Time

Breakfast usually consists of soybean milk and fried dough sticks called *youtiao* (YU-tiao). Lunch is a simple meal of rice or porridge with pickled vegetables or fermented bean curd. Dinner is the main meal, and all the dishes are served at once. Each person has a bowl of rice, and he or she selects food from the communal dishes with a pair of chopsticks or a spoon. Bones or shells are left on the table.

Above: **People enjoy snacking between meals, and the streets are full of vendors selling hot, cold, sweet, or salty snacks.**

"HAVE YOU EATEN?"

The Chinese have a saying, "fortune enters through the mouth," and indeed they delight in eating for pleasure and as a social event. Birthdays, business deals, family gatherings, and festivals are always celebrated with a meal. Their love of food can be seen in their greeting, "Have you eaten?" when two or more Chinese meet. This is equivalent to the Western "Hello."

A CLOSER LOOK AT CHINA

Tea, paper, and fireworks — these are just a few of the contributions China has made to the world. Today, there are fifty-five million ethnic Chinese living in more than one hundred countries. China's positive contributions in areas such as science, technology, and medicine are immeasurable, although some Chinese secret societies have intrigued and struck fear in people worldwide. You have read an overview of China's geography, history, and lifestyle in the previous section. Now, the spotlight falls on some important, specific aspects of this vast country with a long and checkered history.

The lifestyle and outlook of Chinese people has been greatly influenced by Confucianism, a Chinese philosophy named after its founder. But newer thinking has also come about, and the life of women, for example, has greatly improved since the days of foot-binding, when women were confined to the home.

Several major historical movements have shaped modern China — the May Fourth Movement, the Great Leap Forward, the Cultural Revolution, and most recently, economic reforms. Momentous events such as the 1997 return of Hong Kong to China by the British, the killing of demonstrators in Tiananmen Square in 1989, and the Tibet issue will be examined more closely, as will the problems surrounding the construction of the Three Gorges Dam.

Above: **A theme park in Shenzhen, one of China's new economic zones.**

Opposite: **Shanghai's famous waterfront called The Bund, flanked by modern skyscrapers.**

The Art of Healing

For thousands of years, the Chinese have believed that the natural world possesses two qualities: *yin* (YIN) and *yang* (YANG). Yin is represented by femininity, cold, and water. Yang is represented by masculinity, heat, and fire. The yin and yang forces are opposites: female and male, cold and hot, moon and sun, night and day, decay and growth. Yin and yang are not static, but always in motion, just as day follows night. A boy is more yang than yin, and a girl more yin than yang, but nothing is all yang or all yin.

In addition, a vital energy, or *qi* (CHEE) is believed to pervade all matter, including the human body. A person has

Below: **Exotic ingredients on sale at a medicinal market may include deer antlers, tortoise shells, snake gall, and pearl powder. Together with a large variety of herbs, they form an important part of the Chinese system of health care.**

several qi systems, both yin and yang. Yin systems store qi, while yang systems distribute it. The heart, liver, and spleen are yang systems. A person falls ill when the balance of qi in the body is upset. For example, when a person drinks an iced drink, it may make the stomach too yin, and result in a stomachache. A lack of qi in the heart may lead to a feeling of tiredness all the time, while an imbalance in a person's liver qi may cause a severe headache.

A Chinese physician examines a patient by checking his or her general appearance, including the tongue; listening to the breathing and to sounds such as coughing; and taking note of the breath or body odor. The physician asks about the patient's medical history and present symptoms, then takes the patient's pulse to determine the state of the qi systems. After the physician has made a diagnosis, for example, that an elderly woman patient's rheumatism in the knee is caused by a blockage of qi in the knee and the presence of too much yin energy in the body, a combination of herbs will be prescribed to clear the blockage and to increase yang energy in the body. There may be as many as twenty kinds of herbs; they are prepared by being boiled and simmered over a slow fire for several hours. Boiling removes toxins from the herbs and sterilizes the

Below: **The aim of Chinese herbal medicine is to maintain the correct yin-yang balance. Deer antlers on sale at this market are regarded as having a yin property. The antlers are scraped with a sharp instrument; the shavings are then prepared with water and herbs, and the liquid is consumed.**

mixture. Sometimes, these herbs come in the form of a powder or a pill, or they are made into an ointment for application. Some Chinese physicians specialize in acupuncture, which involves inserting fine needles through the skin to regulate the flow of qi to correct any imbalance. But the traditional Chinese system of healing does not include cutting into the body, which is considered a drastic measure. In China today, there are both Western-trained doctors and Chinese physicians, and people go to both.

Confucius, the Philosopher

Confucius, whose philosophy has influenced the Chinese, Japanese, Koreans, and Vietnamese for thousands of years, was born in 551 B.C. He lived in a period of turmoil, when many states fought against each other for power. While working in the accounting offices of a rich landowner in the state of Lu, he studied old texts and learned music. He believed that people had to rediscover the practices of the past so that peace and order could be restored in the country.

He said, "We know so little about how to live in this life that there is no point in worrying about what may happen to us after death. First let us learn to live the right way with other men, and then let whatever happens next take care of itself." He taught how the right relationships between people should be maintained: the ruled should obey the ruler, the son should obey his father, the wife should obey her husband, and the younger brother should obey his elder brother. The only equal relationship was that between friends.

Below: **A Taoist temple in Jiangsu province, built in Confucius' honor. The Taoist philosophy pays tribute to a range of gods and demigods. Some are celestial beings, some are mythical characters, and others are individuals elevated from the status of mere mortals because of their brave deeds or outstanding contributions to society.**

Women were considered inferior to men, and a woman was expected to obey her father as a child, her husband as an adult, and her son in her old age. On the other hand, it was a moral obligation of the person in authority to be just and reasonable. Thus, the father should be kind, but at the same time deal severely with his son's faults. The son should show respect to his parents. This concept of respect should be extended to the state and to society.

Confucius placed great emphasis on learning and encouraged the arts, including music. He also stressed the five virtues of *ren* (RERN), or humanity; *yi* (YI), righteousness; *li* (LI), propriety; *zhi* (jirh), wisdom; and *xin* (SIN), trustworthiness. Everyone should strive ultimately to become a *junzi* (JOON-jir), or superior human — one who is noble in his or her private life and a humble public servant in his or her professional life.

Confucius died in 479 B.C. at the age of seventy-two. His philosophy became popular during the Han dynasty, when scholars had to study his teachings if they wanted to join the government service. Even today, his influence can be seen among the Chinese in their care and respect for the aged, their emphasis on education, respect for principle, and their stress on society before self.

Above: Confucian teaching places much emphasis on education, the need for loyalty, and respect for parents and elders. These kindergarten children are posing for a group photograph.

STIFLING THE SPIRIT OF ENTERPRISE

Confucius' teachings centered mostly on proper social behavior. But his teachings have also been criticized for holding back social progress and scientific thought, stifling the spirit of enterprise and adventure, and promoting the subjugation of women.

Economic Reforms

In 1975, Zhou Enlai, the prime minister of China, announced his plan to modernize the country. However, he died a year later, and it was left to Deng Xiaoping, another Chinese leader, to carry out these reforms. Agriculture, the most important sector in the Chinese economy, was the first to be affected. To encourage farmers to produce more, a new system replaced the commune. Land was now contracted to people according to the size of their households. Farmers had to deliver a certain portion of their harvest to the government, but they could keep any extra produce and sell it on the free market for profit.

To increase agricultural yields, farmers used large amounts of chemical fertilizers and pesticides, which damaged the soil. The land suffered despite good weather in the early 1980s and record harvests. Communal facilities such as irrigation systems fell into disrepair because there was no one to organize people to maintain them. Farmland was also being used for rural factories. As a result, China had to import grain. To remedy some of the problems, the government began a program to improve irrigation and drainage, reclaim wasteland, and introduce new farming techniques.

Below: **The government's new economic policies, aimed at attracting foreign capital and technology, have played an important role in the building of a modern country.**

Above: **Immigrants from the countryside arrive in the big cities to look for work, but many stay homeless and jobless, and are left pondering their fate.**

In industry, state-owned companies were made responsible for their own profits and losses, and were given freedom to hire their workers. They began to reward workers according to the amount of work done instead of paying everyone the same wage. As part of the country's reforms, people were encouraged go into business for themselves, as taxi-drivers, shopkeepers, or stallholders. Technical and vocational education was emphasized to produce a pool of skilled workers. Large numbers of students were sent abroad to study; unfortunately, many chose to remain overseas instead of returning home after graduation. To speed up economic growth and the import of foreign technology, China welcomed foreigners. Foreign investors could set up joint venture firms in special economic zones where they were given privileges, such as low or no taxes, to make it attractive for them to operate.

While such reforms have meant a richer and more modern country, there are many problems as well. The gap between the rich and the poor has grown; those who live on fertile lands or in major industrial centers have become richer, while others who live in less productive areas still struggle to earn a living. In spite of this and other setbacks, the government remains committed to the economic reforms, and made them part of the constitution in 1997.

OPENING DOORS

Besides modernizing farms to improve the living conditions for rural people, the government aims to increase literacy rates in the countryside. It is also strengthening its anti-corruption laws and will continue with its open-door policy of welcoming foreigners to trade with and invest in China.

Holding Up Half the Sky

How sad it is to be a woman!
Nothing on earth is held so cheap.
No one is glad when a girl is born;
By her the family sets no store.

This poem, written in A.D. 3 by Fu Xuan, sums up the life of a woman in old China. Chinese life centered on the farm, and strong hands were needed in the fields; therefore, the Chinese favored sons over daughters. Also, sons took care of their parents in their old age, while daughters left the home when they married to become a member of their husbands' family. Daughters were therefore treated as no more than a temporary possession. Some were sold as babies when their families needed the money, to be brought up as household servants or as prostitutes in another place. At other times, baby girls were drowned at birth.

From the age of seven, a girl's feet were bound tightly to prevent them growing normally, because men liked their wives to have small feet. Her marriage was arranged for her, and after marriage, she lived under the thumb of her mother-in-law. If she failed to produce a son, her husband might take another wife. She could not own property, could not divorce her husband, and if her husband died before her, could not remarry.

It was not until the nineteenth century that Chinese women began to break free from their subservient life and seek equality with men. Western missionaries started schools for girls, and

THE PRACTICE OF FOOT-BINDING

This was a painful practice that stunted the normal growth of feet; girls from wealthy families had to undergo the process from early childhood. With tiny feet to support her weight, a woman could only walk a few small steps at a time, giving her a gait described as that of a swaying willow tree. Small feet were thus regarded as a beauty asset. Peasant women did not have their feet bound because they needed to work in the fields. In 1901, a Manchu emperor finally issued an order banning foot-binding.

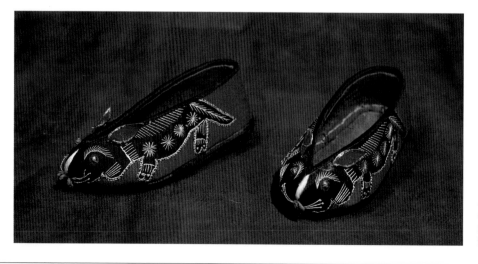

Left: A hand-embroidered shoe for a woman's small, tightly bound foot.

WOMEN GIVEN MORE RIGHTS

Soon after the communists took over China in 1949, they put in place a marriage law that gave women the right to choose their own husbands, file for divorce, and inherit property. Women were also given equal status at home and in the workplace.

Left: **Chinese weight-lifter Zhao Xiali broke world records in various categories in the 1993 Seventh World Women's Weightlifting Championships.**

Western ideas began to influence Chinese intellectuals. In 1901, foot-binding was banned, and in the early 1900s, the Chinese themselves started schools for girls. In 1919, educated Chinese women took part in the movement to modernize China. Many joined the Chinese Communist Party because it was committed to equal rights for women. During the Great Leap Forward in the 1950s, Mao Zedong gave women equality with men, saying that they "held up half of heaven." Women were urged to work in the fields and in factories together with men. Child care centers were set up so children could be taken care of while their mothers worked, and greater attention was paid to women's health problems.

Today, there are women doctors, teachers, scientists, musicians, painters, writers, entrepreneurs, and bus and taxi drivers. China has also produced world-class women sports champions. Many women even go overseas to work as teachers, nurses, or factory workers.

Inventions and Discoveries

The China of today lags behind the rest of the world in science and technology, but this was not always the case. China was the first country to use paper money, and it also invented the fingerprint system of identification. In A.D. 132, the Chinese built the world's first seismoscope to detect earthquakes. They were responsible for the development of the mechanical clock, and in 1088, used an automatic clock drive for an astronomical instrument, long before the Europeans did so in the nineteenth century. Sophisticated astronomical instruments, developed in the thirteenth century, enabled the Chinese to calculate the solar year to an accuracy within twenty seconds. The Chinese consider paper, printing, the compass, and gunpowder their greatest inventions.

Craftsmen invented paper in the first century B.C., but it was only introduced to the royal court in A.D. 105 by a eunuch, Cai Lun, who took credit for the invention. Before that, the Chinese had written on silk or bamboo strips bound together like a venetian blind. The early Chinese used tree bark and hemp to make paper, boiling the materials and then pounding the mixture into pulp before

INNOVATION AT WORK

The Chinese conducted the first population census during the Han dynasty (206 B.C.–A.D. 220), and the French took the idea to the West in the seventeenth century. Other Chinese inventions include porcelain, the winnowing machine, and the washboard.

Left: Seals, with engraved symbols or names, have traditionally been used as a form of endorsement or signature on documents.

laying it on bamboo screens to dry. It was another six hundred years before the use of paper was passed on to the West.

With the traditional practice of writing on paper and the making of seals, it was only a matter of time before the Chinese progressed to printing. Woodblock printing first appeared in the eighth century; pictures and words were carved on blocks of wood, inked, and pressed onto paper. Later, woodblock printing was used to print the first paper money. In the eleventh century, movable type was used; this consisted of single words carved on individual blocks of wood that were reused in different combinations according to need.

About two thousand years ago, the Chinese discovered that a piece of natural magnetite always pointed in a north-south direction, but people began using the compass only in the eleventh century. At first it was used to determine the orientation of buildings, but was later employed in navigation. In the fifteenth century, the Chinese used the compass on sea voyages that took them as far as East Africa.

The invention of gunpowder happened by accident, when a Chinese alchemist was experimenting to make an elixir. Although the Chinese started using gunpowder to make firearms in the eleventh century, its use was not well developed at that point. Instead, gunpowder was used to make fireworks for special occasions, such as the Lunar New Year.

Above: **Modern fireworks display during the Lunar New Year. Matteo Rici, a Jesuit priest who visited China in the sixteenth century, claimed that one fireworks display he saw used enough gunpowder to fight a big war lasting several years.**

HOW NOT TO MAKE GUNPOWDER

The earliest documents on gunpowder were not on how to make it, but on how to avoid making it, probably because of its destructive power.

May Fourth Movement

After the fall of the Qing dynasty in 1911, China became politically divided, with warlords and a weak central government fighting for control. As a result, the country was unable to prevent foreign intervention in its affairs. At the Paris peace conference held at the end of World War I in 1919, the Treaty of Versailles gave the German concessions in Shandong to Japan, instead of transferring them back to the Chinese. On May 4, 1919, three thousand students at Beijing University marched to protest against the treaty and to demonstrate against foreign intervention. Some of the students were arrested, and this sparked a boycott of Japanese goods.

The protest soon spread to other cities, and workers joined in. As a result of public pressure, the Chinese government refused to sign the Versailles treaty. This May Fourth Movement gave impetus to a modernization drive that had begun three years before, in 1916. By that time, China had become impoverished by

Below: **By early this century, China had become impoverished, and most of the people lived in cramped conditions. This situation still persists in the poorer rural areas.**

wars, civil strife, and misrule, and ravaged by natural disasters; it had become the "sick man of Asia."

This modernization movement, started by a small group of intellectuals, was aimed at saving the decaying country by rejecting feudal practices and freeing people's minds from traditional ways. It encouraged the study of Western ideas on democracy, science, and nationalism. In literature, it promoted the usage of the language of the common people.

After May 4, 1919, Western influences became stronger in China, with translations of Western works becoming more numerous. Young people, inspired by the Russian revolution and the establishment of the Soviet Union in 1917, studied socialism and later formed the leadership for the communist revolution in the 1930s and 1940s.

Soon, workers organized themselves into unions that looked after their welfare and fought against the exploitation of workers. When the Chinese Communist Party was set up in 1921, the labor movement became linked with the communists' revolutionary nationalist movement. The workers fought for better working conditions and to free their country from foreign exploitation.

Above: **There were few educated women during the early days of the communist uprising, but they took part in the communist movement in the hope of building a new country. They also began to speak out against the oppression of Chinese women. Today's women play an important role in the country's economy.**

The Lost Years

The Great Leap Forward

Land reform after the communist takeover in 1949 gave land to individual farmers, but the farmers shared farming tools, farmed the land collectively, and shared the harvest. These farming cooperatives proved successful, but the government felt that bigger organizations were needed to speed up agricultural growth, and to build dams and irrigation networks. A new campaign, called the Great Leap Forward, was started in 1957 to achieve this.

Instead of individual ownership of plots of land, all peasants now pooled their land and were organized into large communes of up to fifty thousand people each. Meanwhile, rural industries were set up, but many failed because they lacked proper equipment. To make things worse, these industries drew people away from the farms, and the fields became neglected, leading to a decline in crop production. At the same time, the worst drought in one hundred years hit northern and central China. What followed was a two-year famine that killed about thirty million people.

Below: **Rural workers being mobilized for big public works projects, such as irrigation and terracing.**

Cultural Revolution

In the 1960s, just as China was recovering from the effects of the Great Leap Forward, it was plunged into another era of chaos and confusion, the Cultural Revolution. Begun in 1966, it aimed to change people's traditional values, and Mao Zedong called for an attack against old ideas, customs, culture, and habits. Teachers, engineers, doctors, and other professional people were sent to the countryside to learn from the peasants. Political studies were organized for students and workers. Without teachers, the schools soon stopped functioning. Groups of young people, known as the Red Guards, traveled in large groups throughout the country on buses and trains without paying fares. They destroyed old buildings, temples, and historical artifacts wherever they went. They went into the homes of people they suspected of not supporting the revolution, beat them up, and destroyed their belongings; many were killed or driven to suicide. In 1968, the army was sent to stop the mass destruction. But it was not until 1976, when Mao Zedong died, that the Cultural Revolution came to an end. By then, young people had lost ten years of education, and the country had suffered economically, falling farther behind the rest of the world in science and technology.

Above: **After the failure of the Great Leap Forward movement, communes were scaled down into more manageable sizes, and better farming methods were introduced.**

Midnight Handover

At the stroke of midnight on July 1, 1997, the British flag, the Union Jack, was lowered for the last time in Hong Kong, and the red and yellow flag of China was raised, marking the return of Hong Kong to mainland China after 155 years of British rule.

It was in 1842, after losing the first Opium War to the British, that the Chinese were forced into signing the humiliating Treaty of Nanking. Hong Kong, a small island in southern China, was among the many Chinese possessions awarded to the British as part of the settlement to end the war. Hong Kong has an excellent harbor, and under British rule the colony prospered as a trading post. It grew to become an important port and financial center, with a population of 6.4 million people. From time to time, however, Chinese resentment against the British surfaced, and there were indirect reminders to the British that they were in a "borrowed place on borrowed time" with a "borrowed people."

Talks between Britain and China about Hong Kong's status began in the early 1980s, culminating in the Sino–British Joint Declaration, which agreed that on July 1, 1997, Hong Kong would return to China under a "one country, two systems" principle. It would come under Chinese rule, yet be allowed to keep its existing

Above: **China's Communist Party insignia being erected on a government office building in Hong Kong on July 1, 1997, the day the former British colony was returned to Chinese rule.**

Left: **The British government insignia being taken down from a government building on July 1, 1997, signaling the end of the British era in Hong Kong.**

Left: **A busy street in Causeway Bay, Hong Kong. The island prospered during the period of British rule because of a stable government and the local people's spirit of enterprise.**

freedoms, and judicial and financial systems, at least until the year 2047. Many Hong Kong Chinese emigrated before the handover because of uncertainty over their future under communist-led China. It is estimated that half a million people left Hong Kong between 1984 and 1997 for countries such as the United States, Canada, Australia, and Singapore. The Chinese government hopes to use Hong Kong as a model for its reunification with Macau, a small Portuguese colony, and, possibly, with Taiwan. Taiwan's breakaway occurred in 1949, when the existing Chinese government fled to the island after clashes with the communist troops on the Chinese mainland.

The Origin of Tea Drinking

Drinking tea began in China nearly five thousand years ago. Legend has it that the mythical emperor Shen Nong was visiting a distant region of his empire one summer day when he and his attendants stopped to rest. As his servants were boiling some water to drink, a gust of wind blew some dried leaves from a nearby bush into the pot. The emperor took a sip of the brown liquid and found it refreshing, and so tea drinking began!

Tea drinking first spread from China to Japan, where it was elevated into an art in the form of the tea ceremony. In the 1600s, tea was introduced to Europe and became highly fashionable in France and Holland. In England, the custom of afternoon tea developed, in which sandwiches, scones, and cakes were served with tea. In the 1600s, the Dutch brought tea to their North American colony, New Amsterdam (later New York).

Below: **A tea shop in Beijing. In China, tea is drunk at all times of the day instead of water.**

DIFFERENT BLENDS

Tea is now grown in many parts of the world, including India, Sri Lanka, and Malaysia. There are many ways of preparing tea leaves, which come from the camellia plant, a genus of tropical shrub. Black tea, which has been fermented, yields a hearty, amber brew. Some popular black teas are English Breakfast, Darjeeling, and Orange Pekoe. Black tea blends are sometimes flavored with fruit or spiced. Green tea is from leaves dried by frying or smoking, has a delicate taste, and is light green or golden in color. Favored mainly by the Japanese, green tea is gaining popularity because scientific research shows that it reduces the risk of getting cancer. Oolong tea is a cross between black and green tea.

Today, people around the world drink tea in many ways: with or without sugar or milk, spiced or flavored with fruit, iced or hot, in loose leaves or bagged. An American made the first iced tea in 1904 at the St. Louis World's Fair. The tea merchant, Richard Belchynden, was giving away free samples of hot tea that nobody wanted because of a heat wave. In desperation, he dumped a load of ice into his tea and served the first iced tea. Four years later, another tea merchant, Thomas Sullivan of New York, put samples of tea in little cloth bags to give to restaurants. Instead of taking the tea out of the bags, the restaurants simply threw the bags into their tea pots; thus the tea bag was born.

Overseas Chinese

Apart from the 1.2 billion Chinese who live in China today, there are another fifty-five million ethnic Chinese living in more than one hundred countries — from Canada to Brazil, from England to South Africa, and from Japan to New Zealand. Many were born in the countries in which they live, while some are new immigrants, not only from mainland China, but also from Taiwan and Hong Kong.

The first Chinese to leave China were traders, who traveled to the South Seas or Nanyang (their term for Southeast Asia) during the Song dynasty (960–1279). They sailed in huge ocean-going boats known as junks. In the sixteenth century, the Chinese sailed to Manila in the Philippines to trade with the Spanish, and to Java in Indonesia to trade with the Dutch. From Java, some of the Chinese went to work in Dutch cinnamon gardens in Sri Lanka and on farms on the Cape of Good Hope in Africa. Some Chinese merchants also settled in Siam, which is today's Thailand.

During the nineteenth century, poverty drove many young men to leave their families in China to work as laborers in faraway lands.

Above: **China-born actress Joan Chen has acted in several American movies and now lives in the United States.**

Below: **A bustling street in San Francisco's Chinatown, which has grown to become more than just a Chinese enclave.**

Above: **Chinese quarter in Manhattan, New York.**

They worked as gold miners in North America, sugar-plantation laborers in Cuba, stevedores in Singapore, and rickshaw pullers in India. These workers lived together in ghettos called Chinatowns and organized themselves into associations to take care of their needs. After making enough money, many Chinese immigrants would return home, but some chose to stay and sent for their wives and children. Others married local women. Many descendants of these early settlers have lost much of their Chinese cultural roots, adopting the ways of the local people and speaking the language of their new country.

In the early twentieth century, some Chinese continued to leave their homeland to escape poverty. Others left after the communist takeover in 1949 to escape the communist regime. Many of those who left during and shortly after 1949 were wealthy people, including bankers and businessmen. After 1978, many Chinese students went abroad to study, and many chose not to return. Today, rich, overseas Chinese are helping China's economic reforms by investing billions of dollars in joint venture companies. They have also helped by building schools, roads, and other infrastructure projects in their ancestral hometowns.

Secret Societies

Drug trafficking, the smuggling in of illegal Chinese workers, and gang fights in Chinatown — these are just some of the activities associated with Chinese secret societies in the United States, Canada, Europe, and other parts of the world. So what are secret societies, how did they come about, and why do members, who are mainly men, address each other as "brother?"

Secret societies have existed in China for a very long time. Young men and women, discontented with their poverty, sometimes turned to committing crimes against landlords and government officials. They gathered into groups, opposed the rigid Confucian practices that prevailed, and made their own rules based on loyalty, righteousness, equality, and patriotism. From secret hideouts in forests, they committed armed robbery and piracy, attacked government buildings and government convoys carrying valuable goods, and kidnapped the children of rich families for ransom. They usually robbed only the rich, and sometimes gave part of their loot to the needy. Members of secret societies paid with their lives if they broke any of the oaths they took, which included being loyal to the group and keeping society codes secret.

In times when people were highly oppressed or exploited by those in power, secret societies led peasants in revolts against the government. For example, it was the White Lotus Society that overthrew the Mongols to start the Ming dynasty (1368–1644). In the late 1600s, five monks from China's Shaolin Temple set up a secret society in southern China to overthrow the Qing rulers and restore the Ming dynasty. In modern times, secret societies lent their support to Sun Yat-sen's revolution, which overthrew the Qing dynasty in 1911.

Secret societies drew inspiration from folk literature; for example, the vows made by members were similar to those made in the historical novel, *Romance of the Three Kingdoms*. In it, three men became "sworn brothers" in a peach garden, promising to lay down their lives for one another. One of these men, Liu Bei, said: "Brothers are like one's limbs, but wives like one's clothing," meaning that brothers could not be replaced, but wives could. To this day, vows taken by secret society members are known as "peach garden vows."

Above: **This Chinese secret society membership seal has been stamped with various imprints made to look like the seals of Chinese trading companies. The purpose of doing this is to mislead government authorities.**

One important concept of the secret society is that all members are brothers, with heaven as the father and earth as the mother. Although members are still called "brothers," a reflection of the Chinese patriarchal society, there are also female gang members, or even all-women gangs. The secret society structure broke away from the rigid hierarchy of the mainstream Confucianist society, and women were treated as equals. This relationship of heaven, earth, and humans also led to secret societies being known as triads.

While secret societies drew references from folk literature, they, in turn, inspired writers. One such novel on the exploits of a secret society during the Song dynasty (960–1279) has been translated into English under various titles such as *All Men Are Brothers*, *The Water Margin*, and *Outlaws of the Marsh*. Secret societies were influenced by this book too, and often borrowed titles and slogans.

The Chinese took their secret societies wherever they went, and there are worldwide organizations today. They are not only involved in illegal activities such as drug trafficking, gambling, extortion, prostitution, and moneylending, but also in legitimate business. They own restaurants, are in the real estate business, and finance movies. They have also tried to become involved in politics. One secret society leader in the United States said he donated millions to a political candidate to help ease Chinese immigration into the country.

Left: **An altar table used by secret societies in their initiation ceremony for new members.**

The Silk Road

The fabled Silk Road stretched for 4,350 miles (7,000 km), from the ancient Chinese capital of Changan (today's Xi'an in Shaanxi province) in the east, to the eastern shores of the Mediterranean in the west. It was a treacherous trade route that passed through the shifting sands of the great Takla Makan Desert and crossed high mountain passes. However, merchants persisted because there were fortunes to be made traveling this road.

The Silk Road first became a link between East and West during the Han dynasty about two thousand years ago. Chinese silk, porcelain, iron, lacquer, jade, bronze, and other goods moved west to the great Roman empire, while horses, glass, gold, perfume, and ivory came east to China.

The significance of the Silk Road extended beyond trade. Buddhism from India and Christianity from the West were brought to China via this road. Other arts and cultures also found their way to China and became infused with Chinese culture. The route declined in importance when sea travel became easier and

Below: **Remains of an ancient city along the old Silk Road. The area has been deserted for more than six hundred years. Marco Polo, the Italian traveler, took the Silk Road to China in 1271.**

The Silk Road had many branches that passed through major trading centers. Merchants did not usually travel the entire journey, but sold their goods to other merchants along the route. During the Yuan dynasty, the Mongols extended the Chinese empire to Persia, and the Silk Road became an important means of communication between different parts of the vast empire.

Left: An Uighur man of Xinjiang province engaged in traditional silk weaving. Traders traveled to China to buy the fine, smooth fabric but silk production remained a Chinese secret for many years. Only the Chinese knew that silk was made from the cocoons of tiny silkworms. The Europeans eventually learned the secret, but Chinese silk was still highly sought-after for its beauty and fine quality.

safer; it later fell into disuse. Today, most of the travelers along the old route are tourists, but trade is picking up again, much of it between the new Central Asian republics, such as Kazakhstan and Uzbekistan, and the Chinese in Xinjiang province. A railway line, the Eurasian Continental Bridge, is being built along the road to link the Chinese east coast to Rotterdam in the Netherlands. Thus, an iron caravan will replace the camel caravans of the past.

Three Gorges Dam

In late 1994, after seventy-five years of debate and amid great controversy, work finally began on what will be the world's largest and most powerful dam. When completed in 2009, the Three Gorges Dam will straddle the Yangtze, the world's third largest river. It will be located near a legendary stretch of gorges formed by majestic limestone cliffs. The Three Gorges Dam will stretch 1.3 miles (2 km) across and soar 617 feet (188 m) high, creating behind it a reservoir 413 miles (664 km) long.

First suggested in the 1920s by Sun Yat-sen, the father of modern China, the dam is being built to serve three purposes: to control the floods that kill many people and destroy property every year; to provide hydroelectric power to fuel industrial centers; and to deepen the upper reaches of the Yangtze, slow down the river flow, and widen shipping lanes so that more and bigger ships can travel farther inland. Experts from other countries have helped the Chinese in their decision to build the dam. The Americans first helped the Chinese select a site and the Russians helped in feasibility studies. In the 1980s, a Canadian study team advised that the dam be built.

Some experts, however, have warned that the dam will be an environmental disaster. They fear it will upset the ecology of the river, endanger the habitat of marine life, and deplete commercial fish stocks. It will also deprive agricultural lands along the river of the water and rich silt they receive in the annual floods. Thus, it threatens the livelihood of seventy-five million people who live by farming or fishing along the river's banks. Critics also worry that wastewater discharged into the reservoir will pollute the slow-moving water and that sediment will accumulate behind the dam. Some fear the dam will actually put more people at risk from flooding. Raising the water level behind the dam means that more than a million people will be displaced, plant and animal life will be threatened, and many historical sites will be submerged.

Despite warnings, criticisms, and suggested alternatives, the Chinese government decided to go ahead. Evacuation of people affected by the dam began in 1992. A total of 1.2 million people, mostly farmers, will have to move. Only a small number of farmers will be given new land to continue farming. Many others will have to move into urban areas, away from their traditional way of life.

Above: **Construction of the towering, concrete Three Gorges Dam will affect farmers who live along the river bank. The soil on their land will be deprived of rich silt from the annual flooding of the Yangtze River.**

Opposite: **The Yangtze River gorges in Hubei have inspired Chinese poets and painters through the ages.**

Tiananmen Square Incident

Tiananmen Square in Beijing has been described as the world's biggest public square; it can hold up to one million people. It was originally a palace square in the feudal era, but has since been expanded and is now 123 acres (50 hectares) in size. To the north of the square lies the gate to the Forbidden City, where the emperor used to live. To the west is the Great Hall of the People, where the National People's Congress meets yearly.

Above: **A boy holds a Chinese flag in Tiananmen Square.**

A large portrait of Mao Zedong is displayed prominently within the square, and the place is popular with foreign and local visitors. China's National Day celebrations on October 1 take place at the square, with mass formation dances and fireworks displays.

Tiananmen means "Gate of Heavenly Peace," but the events that have taken place there have not always been peaceful, and many have become milestones in Chinese history. On May 4, 1919, students marched to this square to protest the Treaty of Versailles. It was here on October 1, 1949, that Mao Zedong proclaimed the founding of the People's Republic of China. It was also from this public spot that Mao, in 1966, announced the start of the Cultural Revolution that was to shake the nation. In 1976, public mourning at the square over the death of Prime Minister Zhou Enlai turned into mass protests against the Cultural Revolution.

Demonstrations in 1989

On June 4, 1989, soldiers moved into Tiananmen Square to remove thousands of student demonstrators. This incident was referred to as the Tiananmen Massacre by the Western media. Rising discontent through the 1980s had led up to this tragic day. Economic reforms in the 1980s resulted in smaller student grants, rising prices, and the fear of unemployment among young people. Intellectuals who had expected greater political freedom after the Cultural Revolution were disenchanted with the slow pace of reform. Student demonstrations first started in 1986–1987. Their demands ranged from simple, basic issues such as better food in university cafeterias and a change in lights-out time in dormitories, to more complicated ones such as a faster pace of reform and greater freedom of expression. The authorities did not take strong action against the demonstrators, but only warned against such protests. Soon, intellectuals and students were demanding democracy. Then in April 1989, Hu Yaobang, a reformer who was dismissed from government office, died. Thousands of students converged on Tiananmen Square to pay their respects to Hu and to demand greater political freedom. At first, official response was muted and students continued their protests; they remained defiant even after elder statesman Deng Xiaoping publicly denounced the movement. On May 12, the students went on a hunger strike. Negotiations between student leaders and the government failed. To prevent the situation from deteriorating further, the government ordered the army to clear the square on the night of June 3. Hundreds of people died, among them soldiers sent in to remove the students. China was condemned worldwide for this action, and the United States imposed trade sanctions against the nation. Internally, the incident almost derailed the economic reforms as the rift between reformers and hardliners within the Chinese Communist Party grew. While China has emerged from the dark days of 1989, political freedom remains elusive.

Below: **The 1989 student demonstration in Tiananmen Square.**

Understanding Tibet

Tibet, known to the Chinese as Xizang, sits on the Qinghai-Tibet Plateau in the southwestern part of China. It is about 13,500 feet (4,104 m) above sea level and is crisscrossed by snowcapped mountain peaks. In the lower grasslands, the people live a nomadic life and raise livestock. In the highlands, farmers cultivate a hardy form of barley that grows in cold, dry weather. Potatoes, turnips, apples, rice, and cotton are grown in the warmer river valleys. It is a hard life in a rugged and largely inhospitable terrain.

Tibetans follow a form of Buddhism called Lamaism. They believe in the reincarnation of buddhas, or men who have achieved enlightenment. These buddhas, also known as lamas, come back again and again to live among the people, teach them, and help relieve suffering. The two most important lamas have the titles of Dalai Lama and Panchen Lama.

Tibet first came under Chinese rule during the Yuan dynasty (1271–1368) and again in the early 1700s. In 1911, with the fall of the

Below: **Tibetan followers of Lamaism offer visitors a traditional welcome.**

Above: **Monks from a Tibetan monastery are playing large drums and cymbals as part of a musical performance.**

Qing dynasty, it came under a new Chinese republican government that was very weak; thus, Tibet was left very much on its own. It was only in 1950, after the communists gained power, that China exerted its sovereignty once again and invaded Tibet.

At that time, most Tibetans worked as serfs for monasteries or for the nobility. They paid rent to these landlords for a small plot of land and had to spend part of their time working for the landlords for free. They were also taxed heavily, and when they got into debt had to borrow money at such high interest rates they often could not repay their debts. When this happened, their land was seized and they worked as slaves for the landlords. The Chinese viewed themselves as liberators of the Tibetans from this feudal way of life. At first, the Chinese promised the Dalai Lama control of internal affairs. But when this promise was not met, the Tibetans began to resist communist rule and fighting broke out in 1959. The Dalai Lama had to flee to India, where he still lives in exile.

Tibet became an autonomous region in 1965, which means it has internal self-rule and can maintain its culture, religion, and economic organization. However, economic development depends very much on support from the central Chinese government in terms of money and expertise.

MODERNIZATION OF TIBET

The international community views the modernization of Tibet as a threat to the Tibetans' cultural and religious heritage. It is also viewed as a heavy-handed move and an effort by the Chinese government to undermine Tibetan culture. Even as living conditions improve, these factors continue to cause resentment and friction between the Tibetans and Chinese.

RELATIONS WITH NORTH AMERICA

The first American traders arrived in China in the late eighteenth century. By the mid-nineteenth century, Chinese laborers were also traveling to North America to work in gold mines and on railroads. The United States' interest in China and the Pacific region, however, grew only in the late nineteenth century, with the annexation of the Philippines and Hawaii. Yet, in spite of its relatively late entry, North America has played an important role in modern Chinese history.

Relations with China suffered after the nationalist Kuomintang government fled to the island of Taiwan in 1949. For many years, the United States did not recognize the communist government in China. There has also been public outcry in North America against human rights violations by the Chinese government, notably in the Tiananmen Massacre of 1989. Relations between the two countries have since improved, and the visit of the Chinese president, Jiang Zemin, to the United States in October 1997 may be paving the way for a new era of cooperation. President Jiang also made a three-day state visit to Canada in November 1997.

Above: **An American rally driver gets the attention of curious Chinese during a stopover in a Hong Kong-Beijing car rally.**

Opposite: **A street scene in Beijing reflects an increasing Western influence in China.**

Links Across the Pacific Ocean

The first American trade ship to arrive in China was the *Empress of China*, reaching Guangzhou from New York on August 28, 1784. It had leather and ginseng on board. These were exchanged for tea, ceramic ware, and silk. Chinese people also came to North America in the eighteenth century. The first to arrive were probably ironsmiths and carpenters, taken to western Canada by the British in 1788. There, they helped build a ship, the *West North America*.

The United States and China signed their first commercial treaty, the Treaty of Wanghsia, on July 3, 1844. This was followed by the Treaty of Tientsin in 1858. The extension of the second treaty, known as the Burlingame Treaty, was signed in 1868 and gave the citizens of both countries the right to emigrate freely. In reality, the treaty allowed the Americans to bring huge numbers of Chinese laborers to work in American gold mines and on the railroads. At the time, Canada's foreign relations were managed by the British, its colonial masters, but it also imported huge numbers of Chinese to work on its gold mines and railroads.

In the latter part of the nineteenth century, the Americans' interest in the Pacific region grew after their annexation of the

Below: Chinese bronze, porcelain, and ceramic wares were sought after by North American museums and private collectors as oriental works of art.

Above: **A Chinese worker packs fruit in a Western-style supermarket.**

Philippines and Hawaii. They were also worried that the Europeans were cornering the Chinese market. In 1898, they proposed an "open-door" policy to the Europeans, in which trade within the different European territories in China was made equal for everyone. After the fall of the Qing dynasty in 1911, America was linked closely with the Kuomintang government, and helped fight the Japanese and communists by providing arms, expertise, and money. Their aid extended beyond military; for example, American engineers helped the Chinese select the site for the Three Gorges Dam in the 1940s; and John Dewey, an American educator, helped the Chinese reform their education system.

Conflict with Communist China

When the communists took over China in 1949, the United States maintained its close relations with the Kuomintang government that had fled to the island of Taiwan. The United States refused to recognize the communist government in China. When the Korean War broke out in 1950, China supported North Korea, while the United States supported South Korea. This led to hostilities between the two countries that lasted for twenty years.

The Gold Mountain and Railroads

Famine hit Guangdong province in southeast China in the 1850s; at the same time, gold was discovered in California. Many Chinese men left for the "gold mountain" in America, hoping to strike it rich. They did not intend to live in America, but to return home to their families after they had made their fortune. When gold was discovered in western Canada, many Chinese went there as well. The Gold Rush increased the demand for railroads to link the east coast to the west, and the Chinese provided cheap labor for building these railroads, both in America and Canada.

By the early 1880s, there were three hundred thousand Chinese in America. The railroads had been built and the Chinese were no longer welcome. America faced a period of economic depression following the Civil War and the Chinese were competing with Americans for limited jobs. In 1882, the United States passed the Chinese Exclusion Act restricting Chinese immigration. This law was repealed only in 1943, allowing Chinese men to send for their wives. In 1952, the Chinese in America were allowed to apply for citizenship and in 1965, restrictions on Asian immigration were lifted and more Chinese moved to the United States.

In Canada, anti-Chinese feelings began building up in the late 1800s. With the completion of the railroads, the Chinese were turning to jobs usually held by the Canadians. In 1885, the Canadian government responded by imposing a tax to restrict Chinese immigration. In 1923, it banned Chinese immigration altogether. The ban was lifted in 1947 and that same year Chinese Canadians were given the right to vote in federal elections.

Opposite: **A lion dance in San Francisco, California, where many Chinese have settled over the years.**

Left: **Chinese made up a large part of the labor force that built the railroads in the United States and Canada in the 1800s. One of the hardest sections was the Central Pacific Railroad, which cut through the Sierra Mountains. Deep snows in the winter made the work even harder.**

A New Way of Life

The Chinese in North America are not all on the same cultural wavelength. Some have grandparents who were born in the United States or Canada, who speak little or no Chinese, and for whom some Chinese cultural practices seem quite foreign. Then there are the new Chinese immigrants from China, Taiwan, Hong Kong, or other parts of the world, who sometimes speak little or no English, and whose ways are very different. Some arrive illegally in search of the American dream and usually end up working in sweatshops or in other menial jobs. Others, however, are professionals, businessmen and women, skilled workers, and students.

The Chinese have mostly settled in the coastal areas of North America. In the United States, they are concentrated in California, Washington, and New York, although they also live in Illinois and Arkansas. In Canada, many Chinese live in Vancouver, in British Columbia, and in Toronto. There are so many Chinese in Vancouver

Left: **Chinatown in New York is a place where Chinese can buy Chinese food, Chinese-language newspapers, books, and other items. While many are happily settled in America, other Chinese North Americans, both first-generation and later generations, feel they are discriminated against at work and in their social life.**

that the city has more Chinese-language newspapers than English ones. The Chinese also have their own television and radio stations. Chinese children attend mainstream schools, whether public or private. But some parents send their children to Chinese classes on the weekends so that they do not lose touch with their own culture and language. For newly immigrated children who speak little English, going to school can be traumatic. Not only do they have to cope with learning a new language and following lessons in it, they sometimes also have to face the taunts of their classmates.

The Chinese today are among the best-educated ethnic groups in North America, and many are professionals and skilled workers. They are well represented in the National Aeronautics and Space Administration, in California's Silicon Valley, and in universities and research institutes. Among the six people who programed IBM's Deep Blue, a supercomputer that defeated chess champion Garry Kasparov, there were two Chinese-Americans. Other successful Chinese-Americans are I. M. Pei, an architect who has designed some of the world's major landmarks, including the glass pyramid at the Louvre Museum in Paris; and Amy Tan, a bestselling author. Gary Locke became the first Chinese-American governor of Washington state in 1997, while Raymond Chan is Canada's secretary of state (Asia-Pacific). Successful Chinese-Americans have helped diminish anti-Chinese prejudice in North America.

Above, left: **The architect, I.M. Pei, is world-famous for his work. This picture shows him in his younger days.**

Above, right: **Amy Tan has written several novels. One of her books, *The Joy Luck Club*, has also recently been made into a Hollywood movie.**

North Americans in China

Since China opened its doors to foreign investments in 1979, many American and Canadian companies — including General Motors, Eastman Kodak, DuPont, Northern Telecom, and SMC-Lavalin — have set up businesses in China. With these have come many North American executives and their families. There are also teachers, engineers, architects, scientists, doctors, and other professionals who are usually on one-year contracts in China. They come to gain a better understanding of the Chinese lifestyle and to enrich their own experiences. There are also North American students studying in Chinese universities because they are interested in Chinese culture and language.

There is a small group of North Americans who have devoted most of their lives to China. Many came before the communist takeover in 1949. The first American to obtain Chinese citizenship after the communist takeover was George Hatem, a doctor. In 1933, after graduating from medical school, he went to China to study tropical and venereal diseases. He stayed on and, until his death in 1988, was a world authority on leprosy and public health.

Above: **Chinese president Jiang Zemin's visit to the United States in October 1997 helped to improve ties between the two countries.**

Below: **An American artist draws for some Chinese school-children.**

Forging New Links

In 1970, Canada established diplomatic relations with China, paving the way for other Western countries, including America, to do so. Ties between China and the United States began with American relaxation of travel and trade restrictions, and the visit of a U.S. ping-pong team to China in 1971. In 1972, President Richard Nixon of the United States visited China and met Chinese leader Mao Zedong. Formal diplomatic ties were established in 1979, and trade has grown immensely between China and North America. Billions of dollars of goods are traded across the Pacific Ocean.

Relations between the United States and China are complicated by the issue of Taiwan, but progress is being made. In October 1997, President Jiang Zemin of China traveled to the United States to meet President Bill Clinton of the United States. The two presidents agreed to have more exchanges in science, technology, and education. President Jiang also made a three-day state visit to Canada the following month. China's immediate concern is to complete its process of modernization with continued economic reforms. For the United States, a more developed Chinese market would increase China's ability to take in more American capital and technology.

Above: **Even today, among the many other commodities traded, Chinese silk still finds its way to North America.**

GOODS TRADED

Canada imports mainly garments, toys, and games from China, and exports wheat, wood products, and electronic goods. The United States imports electrical goods, toys, sports equipment, machinery, leather goods, textiles, and garments from China, and exports machinery, cotton yarn, aircraft, fertilizers, cereals, and electronic products.

Taiwan — A Difficult Issue

The issue of Taiwan has placed a strain on the United States' relations with China. When the Kuomintang government was defeated by the communists in 1949, it fled to Taiwan island, where Chiang Kai-shek became the first president of the Republic of China in Taiwan. For a time, it appeared as if the new communist government in China would invade Taiwan. But it decided instead to concentrate on destroying nationalist elements on the Chinese mainland. Over the years, however, the communists have kept up a continued threat to invade the island.

The United States chose to retain ties with the Kuomintang in Taiwan, offering it financial and military backing. When the Korean War broke out in 1950, for example, President Harry Truman of the United States sent an American fleet to patrol the Taiwan Strait and protect Taiwan against a possible Chinese attack. Since then, U.S. relations with China have been strained.

China claims Taiwan as Chinese territory, and its aim is to unify it with the mainland. Meanwhile, Taiwan claims to be the rightful government of China. For almost five decades, Taiwan and mainland China have fought a diplomatic battle, each not recognizing the status of the other. This division between the "two Chinas" has been a sensitive issue, aggravated by the fact that both parties have widely different political, economic, and social agendas. For years, many countries, including the United States, supported Taiwan's stand.

In 1972, however, the United Nations recognized the People's Republic of China on the mainland as the government of China. This decision cost Taiwan its seat in the United Nations. It was around this time that the United States adopted a policy that brought it into a more cordial relationship with China. It established diplomatic ties with China in 1979 and stopped formal links with Taiwan. However, it still sold arms to the island and remained committed to its defense. Meanwhile, Taiwan is increasingly exerting its independence from China, although some Taiwanese claim they want reunification.

In 1995, the United States angered China when it allowed Taiwanese president, Lee Teng-hui, to travel to America. In early 1996, China mounted a big military exercise, as a threat, to coincide with the first presidential election in Taiwan. The United States sent two aircraft carriers to the Taiwan Strait as a warning against Chinese invasion of the island. The United States has also continued to sell arms to Taiwan, and the issue remains a sore point.

Above: **President Lee Teng-hui of Taiwan traveled to the United States in 1995. His visit was criticized by the Chinese government.**

Cultural Connections

The sharing of culture goes both ways between China and North America. Because of the many early Chinese immigrants, Chinese takeout food and restaurants can now be found in any city. North Americans have also been drinking tea, a beverage that first came from China, for more than two hundred years. American fast-food chains such as McDonald's and Kentucky Fried Chicken have become a common sight in Chinese cities. The Chinese have even imitated them, serving similar food in a similar style. Some North Americans like to dress in Chinese silk, sometimes in garments with Mandarin-style collars held together by Chinese buttons. In China, young Chinese wear denim jackets and jeans.

There has been an exchange in the performing arts as well. Americans watch movies made in China and the Chinese watch movies made in Hollywood. While there is no director from mainland China working in the United States yet, film directors from Hong Kong and Taiwan are popular in America, and a few have won acclaim. In China, Chinese rock singers play music composed by North American rock groups, and Michael Jackson is more popular than most Chinese pop singers. Chinese drama companies also stage plays by American playwrights.

Above: **McDonald's fast-food restaurants are a common sight in Beijing and other large Chinese cities.**

FORTUNE COOKIES

Today, Americans of all races order takeout food from Chinese restaurants if they do not want to cook. There is even Chinese food that is uniquely American: fortune cookies and a mixed vegetable dish called chop suey made their start in America.

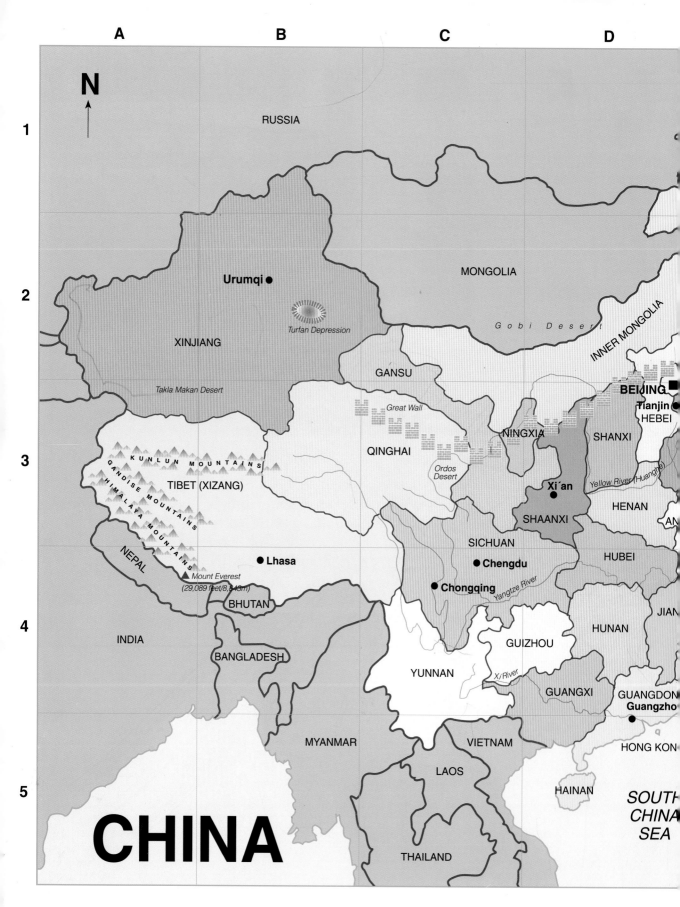

E   F

HEILONGJIANG

JILIN

LIAONING

NORTH
KOREA

SEA OF
JAPAN

SOUTH
KOREA

JAPAN

NDONG

YELLOW
SEA

EAST
CHINA
SEA

JIANGSU

Canal

anjing
● Shanghai

HEJIANG

IAN

men

TAIWAN

	International Boundary
	State Boundary
■	Capital
●	City
	River

Anhui D3

Bangladesh B4
Beijing D3
Bo Hai E3
Bhutan B4

Chengdu C4
Chongqing C4

East China Sea E3
Everest, Mt. A4

Fujian E4

Gandise Mountains A3
Gansu C2
Gobi Desert C2
Grand Canal E3
Great Wall C3
Guangdong D4
Guangzhou D4
Guangxi D4
Guizhou C4

Hainan D5
Hebei D3
Heilongjiang E2
Henan D3
Himalaya Mountains A3
Hong Kong D5
Hubei D4
Hunan D4

India A4
Inner Mongolia D2

Japan F3
Jiangsu E3
Jiangxi D4
Jilin E2

Kunlun Mountains A3

Laos C5
Lhasa B4
Liaoning E2

Mongolia C2
Myanmar B5

Nanjing E3
Nepal A4
Ningxia C3
North Korea E2

Ordos Desert C3

Qinghai C3

Russia B1

Sea of Japan F2
Shaanxi D3
Shandong E3
Shanghai E4
Shanxi D3
Sichuan C3
South China Sea D5
South Korea E3

Taiwan E4
Takla Makan Desert A3
Thailand C5
Tianjin D3
Tibet (Xizang) B3
Turfan Depression B2

Urumqi B2

Vietnam C5

Xi River C4
Xiamen E4
Xi'an D3
Xinjiang A2

Yangtze River C4
Yellow River (Huanghe)
   D3
Yellow Sea E3
Yunnan C4

Zhejiang E4

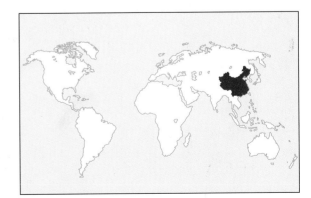

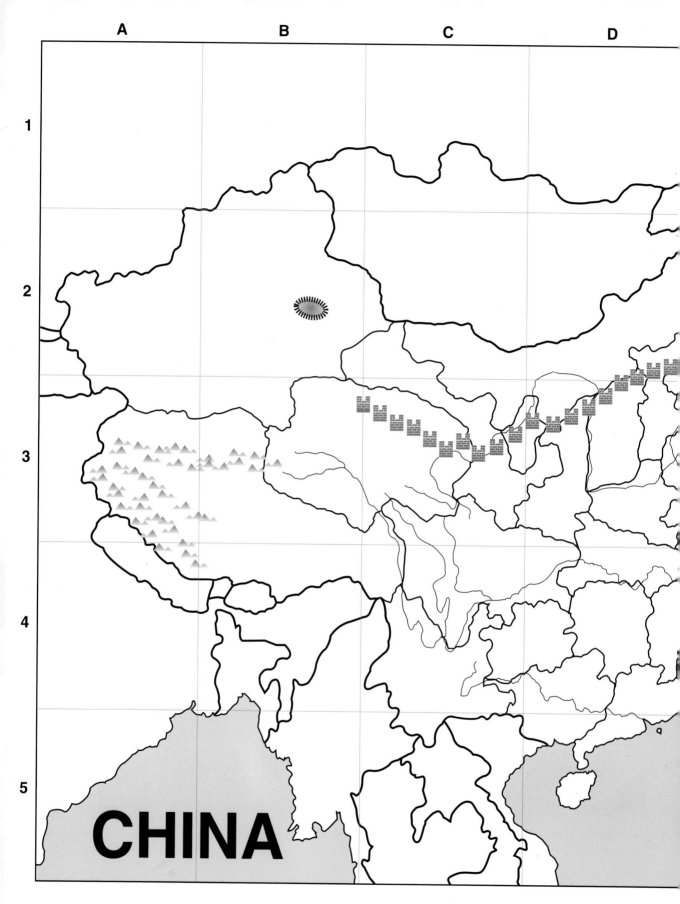

CHINA

E   F

How Is Your Geography?

Learning to identify the main geographical areas and points of a country can be challenging. Although it may seem difficult at first to memorize the location and spelling of major cities or the names of mountain ranges, rivers, deserts, lakes, and other prominent physical features, the end result of this effort can be rewarding. Places you previously did not know existed will suddenly come to life when referred to in world news, whether in newspapers, television reports, or other books and reference sources. This knowledge will make you feel a bit closer to the rest of the world, with its fascinating variety of cultures and physical geographies.

Used in a classroom setting, the instructor can make duplicates of this map using a copy machine (PLEASE DO NOT WRITE IN THIS BOOK!). Students can then fill in any requested information on their individual map copies. Used one-on-one, the student can also make copies of the map on a copy machine and use them as a study tool. The student can practice identifying place names and geographical features on his or her own.

China at a Glance

Land area	3.7 million square miles (9.6 million square kilometers)
Population	1.2 billion
Capital	Beijing
Provinces	Anhui, Fujian, Gansu, Guangdong, Guizhou, Hainan, Hebei, Heilongjiang, Henan, Hubei, Hunan, Jiangsu, Jiangxi, Jilin, Liaoning, Qinghai, Shandong, Shaanxi, Shanxi, Sichuan, Yunnan, Zhejiang
Autonomous Regions	Guangxi, Inner Mongolia, Ningxia, Tibet, Xinjiang
Special Administrative Region	Hong Kong
Major Rivers	Yangtze, Yellow (Huanghe), Xi
Highest Point	Zhumulangma Feng (Mt. Everest); 29,089 feet (8,843 m)
National Language	*Putonghua* (Mandarin)
Major Religions	Taoism, Buddhism, Islam, Christianity
Important Anniversaries	Anniversary of the founding of the People's Republic of China, October 1; Anniversary of the founding of the Communist Party of China, July 1
Important Festivals	Lunar New Year, Mid-Autumn Festival, Tomb-Sweeping Day, Dragon Boat Festival
Famous Leaders	Sun Yat-sen, father of modern China Mao Zedong, founder of communist China Deng Xiaoping, prime mover of economic reforms
Main exports	Textiles, garments, telecommunications and recording equipment, petroleum, minerals
Main imports	Specialized industrial machinery, chemicals, manufactured goods, steel, textiles, yarn, fertilizers
Currency	Renminbi (RMB 8.10 = U.S. $1 as of 1998)

Opposite: **Beautiful flame trees in flower line the banks of this river in China.**

Glossary

Mandarin Words

cai (chai): vegetables.

che (CHERH): vehicle.

fan (FAHN): grain

danwei (TAHN-way): work unit.

gege (KERH-kerh): elder brother.

hongbao (HOHNG-pao): red packets containing gifts of money.

huqin (HOO-chin): a type of violin.

jiejie (JIEH-jieh): elder sister.

junzi (JOON-jir): a superior or noble man.

li (LI): prosperity.

pinyin (PIN-yin): a system of translating Chinese words into romanized script.

pipa (PI-pah): a four-stringed lute.

putonghua (PU-TONG-hua): Mandarin, a northern dialect which is also the national language.

qi (CHI): a form of energy believed to flow through the human body. Acupuncture is a traditional medicinal practiced to regulate the flow of qi.

qigong (CHI-kohng): a breathing exercise that directs energy through the body.

Qingmingjie (CHING-ming jieh): Tomb-Sweeping Day, a traditional rite.

ren (RERN): people or humanity.

taijiquan (TAI-chi-CHUAN): shadow boxing, also practiced as a form of exercise.

tianzi (TIAN-zi): son of heaven, a title held by the Chinese emperor.

wushu (WU-shu): art of self-defense known in the West as *gongfu*.

xi (SI): trustworthiness.

yang (YANG): male, hot, or strong properties; the opposite of *yin*.

yi (YI): righteousness.

yin (YIN): female, cold, or weak properties; the opposite of *yang*.

youtiao (YU-tiao): fried dough sticks.

zhi (JIRH): wisdom.

Zhongqiujie (CHONG-chiu jieh): Mid-Autumn Festival, during which children carry lanterns and everyone eats mooncakes.

English Vocabulary

acrobatics: a spectacular physical performance involving great agility.

alchemist: a medieval chemical scientist aiming to turn base metals into gold.

artifact: an archaeological object; usually an object, tool, or ornament representing a particular culture or stage of technological development.

auspicious: bringing good luck.

brocade: a rich, oriental, silk fabric with raised patterns woven in gold and silver.

commune: a group of farmers that farm the land collectively, share farming tools, and share the harvest. After the communist takeover in China, land was pooled and farmers were organized into communes.

constitution: the basic principles and laws of a nation, state, or social group that determine the powers and duties of the government.

curriculum: the courses offered by an educational institution or the set of courses that result in a specialization.

dam: a barrier built across a body of water to create a reservoir and control the flow of the water.

dragon: a mythical creature believed by the Chinese to embody wisdom and strength. The ancient Chinese believed dragons inhabited lakes and rivers, and also lived among the clouds.

dragon boats: boats with a dragon-head carved on the bow. They participate in races during the dragon boat festival.

drought: a long period of dryness that can cause extensive damage to crops and animals.

dumpling: a small mass of dough cooked by boiling or steaming.

elixir: a substance believed capable of changing base metals into gold; a substance believed to prolong life indefinitely.

embroidery: the art of making decorative designs on cloth with hand or machine needlework.

extortion: the act of obtaining money by force or intimidation.

feasibility: the possibility of something being done or carried out.

fortification: works erected to defend a place or position.

gong: a disk-shaped percussion instrument that produces a resounding tone when struck, usually with a padded hammer.

hydroelectric power: electricity produced by using water power.

irrigation: a system of supplying water to the fields by artificial means.

karaoke: a form of musical entertainment in which a person sings into a microphone to the tune of recorded instrumental music.

Kuomintang: the main political party in China from 1929 to 1949. Its leaders fled to Taiwan in 1949 after their defeat by the communists and, under Chiang Kai-shek, set up a government in Taiwan.

magnetite: a black mineral that is an oxide of iron and has magnetic properties.

mooncakes: small, round cakes filled with lotus seed paste.

municipalities: political units with the powers of limited self-government.

Nestorians: members of a church that separated from Byzantine Christianity after A.D. 431, based in Persia and surviving chiefly in Asia Minor.

Peking Man: an extinct prehistoric man, identified from skeletal remains found in cave deposits in China.

saber: a cavalry sword with a curved blade.

seal: a device engraved with a raised image that is inked and then stamped to produce an emblem or symbol used as evidence of authenticity.

seismograph: a mechanical device used to measure and record vibrations within the earth.

serf: a member of a low feudal class, subject to the will of his or her lord.

stevedore: a person who loads or unloads ships.

sweatshop: a shop or factory in which workers are employed for long hours at low wages and under poor conditions.

warlord: a military commander who exercises civil power by force, usually in a limited area.

yak: a large, long-haired ox found in Tibet and mountainous parts of Central Asia.

zither: an instrument with strings strung over a shallow horizontal soundboard and played with the fingers.

More Books to Read

A Taste of China. Roz Denny (Thomson Learning)

Ancient China. Eyewitness Books series. Arthur Cotterell (Dorling Kindersley)

Ancient China. See Through History series. Brian Williams (Reed Educational and Professional Publishing)

The Ancient Chinese. Look into the Past series. Julia Waterlow (Thomson Learning)

China. Festivals of the World series. Colin Cheong (Gareth Stevens)

Chinese Americans: *Footsteps to America* series. Alexandra Bandon (Macmillan)

Chinese-Americans. Tina Moy (Marshall Cavendish Corporation)

Endangered Animals of the Northern Continents. In Peril series. Barbara Behm and Jean-Christophe Balouet (Gareth Stevens)

Exploration into China. Wang Tao (New Discovery Books)

Journey Through China. Philip Steele (Troll Associates)

Papercrafts Around the World. Phyllis and Noel Fiarotta (Sterling Publishing)

Passport to China. Stephen Keeler (Franklin Watts)

Videos

China and the Forbidden City. (Monterey Home Video distributed by Fries Home Video)

China: A Journey in Pictures. (Presented by Kodak in cooperation with CITS & CAC)

Discovering China and Tibet. (International Video Network)

Web Sites

pasture.ecn.purdue.edu/~agenhtml/agenmc/china/

pasture.ecn.purdue.edu/~agenhtml/agenmc/china/zzodia.html

nis.accel.worc.k12.ma.us/WWW/Projects/China/kidschina.html

www.enchantedlearning.com/subjects/greatwall/

Due to the dynamic nature of the Internet, some web sites stay current longer than others. To find additional web sites, use a reliable search engine with one or more of the following keywords to help you locate information on China. Keywords: *China, Chinese, Confucius, Mao Zedong, Beijing, Sun Yat-sen, Great Wall.*

Index